Charlie's
Thinking
Cheese

A story to stimulate young minds and warm old hearts.

Mark Juarez

Dedicated to Humanity

Charlie's THINKING CHEESE
Copyright © 2010 by Mark Juarez

Written by Mark Juarez with assistance, editing and design by those named
in the acknowledgment
Illustration by: Michael Fravel and Kledy Dongo Pflucker

Library of Congress Cataloging-in-Publication
ISBN 978-0-9703173-0-8
Printed in China

Published by:
The Happy Company
26203 Production Ave. - Suite 4
Hayward, CA 94545
www.thehappycompany.com
www.thinkingcheese.com

First edition

CONTENTS

TO THE READER

I couldn't help digging my fork into that last piece of scrumptiously smooth cheesecake, sliver by sliver. It began with only a tiny urge to taste the dessert one more time. I told myself I would only whittle a thin piece off the side and save the rest for her. Before I knew it, there was an irresistible urge to keep on going! When I finally realized what I had done, the whole slice was gone. I found myself nervously pacing back and forth in the kitchen; the last slice of that cheesecake was supposed to be an implicit reward for a hard day at work. She would be so disappointed to discover it's now gone. I attempted to find salvation in the perfect reason for how the last piece of cheesecake mysteriously disappeared...and voila!

Earlier that day as I was painting the kitchen, I had noticed a small hole in the baseboard next to the refrigerator. Underwhelmed with the monotony of painting and overwhelmed with the guilt of eating the last slice of cheesecake, I decided to have a little fun with this discovery. By painting a little house around the hole with the name "Charlie" above it, I created an endearing story as my alibi for eating the last piece of cheesecake, hopefully sparing my life. With that stroke of creative inspiration, my new friend Charlie the Mouse was created.

To my surprise, even though my story was not very believable, it seemed to go over well and was even cherished. "You're such an adorable dork!" Wow, she wasn't even mad at me! From that day on, Charlie and I could indulge in our favorite foods and enjoy them to our heart's and stomach's content, guilt-free. However, it seemed to go both ways. Or at least it SEEMED like Charlie was beating me to some of my favorite snacks! Charlie became a beloved part of our happy family. We talked so much about Charlie that he began to seem very real—or perhaps he was just my alter ego!

I came up with this story to reflect my faith in humanity and the belief that EVERYTHING in life is an opportunity. Every time something goes wrong, or is unexpected, there's a valuable gift or lesson to be learned. Once I had this realization, I was excited because I was on the lookout for those precious learning opportunities. I could always trust that something great was going to happen and that I would gain wisdom through these experiences. The world is my classroom and I never want to stop being a student.

An excellent example is looking at the plethora of financial and psychological struggles we are currently facing as a nation, and indeed, a world. This is an excellent opportunity to create good things from a terrible situation. With this in mind, I decided to set the story of Charlie BOTH in the Great Depression of the 1930's and the current crisis. I wanted to parallel the eras to draw out the lessons in each period and the opportunities that can grow from that understanding. What might seem like our moment of despair may, in fact, be a great gift, if we just remain open enough to receive it.

I hope this book touches the lives and warms the hearts of all who read it.

-Mark Juarez

Who ate the cheesecake?!

CHAPTER ONE
BROKEN DREAMS OF GRANDEUR

"When the door of happiness closes, another opens; but often we look so long at the closed door that we do not see the one which has been opened for us." – Helen Keller

"Sandy, did you write this note?" Mitch asked as he stood at the kitchen door. "Who's Charlie?"

"Charlie's a mouse," Sandy answered absentmindedly from behind her book. The words slipped out and instantly she realized what she had done. All her plans of how to tell Mitch about Charlie were suddenly irrelevant.

"What are you reading? Whatever it is, you are seriously losing it!" Mitch returned to the sauce simmering on the stove, disregarding the note.

Sandy's eyes were still fixed on the book but her mind no longer comprehended its words. *Why is it so hard to tell him? There was a time when Mitch and I could tell each other anything. What happened to us? I've got to tell him soon. Mitch will certainly encounter Charlie again or put together the signs of a mouse in the house. Charlie could actually be in danger! I'll tell him soon, I will!*

I'll find just the right time.

At that moment, Mitch came back to the living room with a plate of food, turned on the TV and sat down. "Dinner's on the stove. Go dish up," Mitch grunted, grabbing the remote to start channel surfing.

Putting aside her book, Sandy went into the kitchen.

"Spaghetti again," she sighed.

Sandy looked at the kitchen table remembering times when the warm glow of candles and wafts of soft jazz added a special ambiance to their meals together. "Mitch can we eat in the kitchen tonight?" Sandy called.

"Yeah, not much on here anyway," said Mitch, taking the remote and joining her at the table.

"Mitch, I know this has been hard for you. Losing a job is never easy," Sandy began, gentle and concerned.

"I really don't want to talk about it," Mitch retorted.

"I'm just worried about you. My job is secure. We can live off what I make. This cottage is small and cozy—I think we could get used to it. I can only imagine how discouraging it is to be turned down for every executive position you've applied for. Maybe you should look at some other possibilities. You once had a dream of changing the world. I loved it. Maybe you can start by volunteering and some opportunities will open up."

"I can't do that. We'll never get back to where we were on your salary alone. And if I volunteer it will only lead to a low paying non-profit job. We also had dreams of grandeur—I want to make a better life for you Sandy. I've got to stay focused. But I really don't want to talk about this anymore." Mitch ended the conversation by picking up his plate and heading into the living room, remote in hand. Now alone at the table, staring blankly at Mitch's chair, Sandy could feel a tear slowly sliding down her face. She quickly wiped her cheek with the back of her hand and retreated to the couch, escaping into a book she didn't want to read.

Staring at the pages, she thought of how else she might be able to help Mitch. She hated seeing him like this, dejected and longing for their former life. She felt certain that once Mitch met Charlie, everything would be okay. But she had no idea how to tell him without sounding crazy.

Sandy smiled as she remembered the day she realized that Charlie was still with her, even here. A week after they had moved into the cottage, Sandy began to notice food missing from the refrigerator and pantry. It was never a lot, but she had seen the signs before. In fact, she'd grown up with them. The first sign was the missing food. Then came the heartwarming notes written in small curly letters, left in peculiar places along the floorboard, tucked into a crevice, behind the baking mix in the pantry, in the cookie jar, and even on the side of the refrigerator.

When Sandy found the first note in their new home, she quickly penned her response while Mitch was not in the room.

Behind the refrigerator looked like a perfect spot to tuck the little note. With it, she left a little hunk of Swiss cheese, Charlie's favorite.

Hi Charlie!
Glad you came with me. Here's a little cheese for you! Mitch doesn't know about you yet. Be careful! I'll let you know when the coast is clear. I'll try to tell him soon!—Love, Sandy

CHAPTER TWO
MORNING MEMORIES

"We make a living by what we get. We make a life by what we give." – Sir Winston Churchill

The next morning, as Mitch slept, Sandy snuck outside to welcome the early morning sun as it shone across the porch. She glanced around the neighborhood, appreciating the simple peace and the telltale signs of spring arriving. Since she and Mitch had moved into their new cottage, Sandy found refuge in the morning before Mitch woke up; it was her time to reflect on all the changes that had taken place since Mitch got laid off. It was her space from the tension that was gradually building between them.

Mornings were the hardest for Mitch. They were just another reminder that he had to start yet another day in an economy where his dreams, success and accomplishments didn't matter. Having to move to the small cottage had been a rude awakening for him. He felt like a failure for having to move them out of their luxurious, gated community. Sandy's positive outlook since they moved to the cottage made him feel even worse. He couldn't understand why it didn't bother Sandy as much as it bothered him, and he felt very alone in his frustration and misery.

Sandy, on the other hand, was enjoying the refreshing perspective that the new changes had brought. She had grown weary of coming home from work and spending her evenings alone in a large beautiful house while Mitch met with clients. Between their two jobs and their social events, they were constantly running around.

Over the years, she noticed herself losing touch with the simple things that had once brought her happiness, like relaxing on Sunday afternoons on the couch with her husband. She missed them cooking together, laughing as spaghetti sauce splattered their clothes. She even missed their nighttime conversations while crammed into their only available bathroom. Even though Mitch's job had provided very well for them, it still seemed something, everything, was missing.

Sandy had been secretly relieved when they had to downsize and move a few neighborhoods over, despite Mitch's promises that it was only temporary. This place reminded her of her grandfather's home in the country. She had spent innocent summers timelessly wandering the blue-green fields and vibrant, well-kept garden. The flood of smells floating on the gentle breeze across the grass led her back to those summers long ago. She welcomed in the memories - memories of family, of happiness, and of Charlie.

Sandy thought back over her life with Charlie. It had been some time since she had last seen him. He always seemed to pop up when he was most needed and he had been with the family ever since the days of Great Grandfather Henry.

Sandy grew up with Charlie. He was part of the family. It was Charlie who had shown her family how to garden during the struggles of the Great Depression. It was Charlie who had rekindled a sense of abundance during her family's greatest time of need. And it was Charlie who showed them that all was possible.

However, getting someone outside the family to understand that Charlie was a mouse had always proven to be a nearly impossible task. Sandy worried about how to bring up Charlie to Mitch. She knew she would have to. But for now, she allowed herself to linger in the past, in the comfort of her memories and her many family stories.

Words of Wisdom
Charlie's Favorite Quotes

The simplest things are often the truest
– Richard Bach

"With the new day comes new strength and new thoughts." – Eleanor Roosevelt

"The best remedy for those who are afraid, lonely or unhappy is to go outside, somewhere where they can be quiet, alone with the heavens, nature and God." –Anne Frank

"The only limit to our realization of tomorrow will be our doubts of today." – Franklin D. Roosevelt

"In every conceivable manner, the family is link to our past, bridge to our future." – Alex Haley

"Family and friends are hidden treasures; seek them and enjoy their riches." – Wanda Hope Carter

"Everything that is done in the world is done by hope." – Martin Luther

"Memory is a way of holding onto the things you love, the things you are, the things you never want to lose." – Author Unknown

"The deepest principle in human nature is the craving to be appreciated." – William James

14

CHAPTER THREE
THE SMELL OF SOMETHING SINISTER

"I always entertain great hope." – Robert Frost

Sandy remembered very little about Great Grandfather Henry. Black and white photos, yellowing and brittle, and the tales she had been told by her family were the only remnants she carried of him. He passed away while she was still in diapers. The only memories of him she could call her own were his warm brown eyes and the smell of the medicated cream he used, a strong menthol odor that had made her nose wrinkle.

It was Henry who had first officially met Charlie. In those days Henry was a young strapping fellow with a full head of dark hair, which he kept slicked back like Clark Gable. Henry's family, like everyone else in the country at the time, was completely destitute. He had been out of work for months and there were no prospects for work anytime soon. They had no money and very little food. Times were incredibly trying for everyone. But when Charlie arrived, that all changed.

"It's a rat!" Henry's youngest son, Ardy screamed. Henry grabbed a broom and rushed into the boys' bedroom. "Where is it, boys? Rats are filthy creatures. Dirty rodents! I bet these came from the Roberts' place. That place is a pigsty!"

They saw a tiny, gray mouse slip out from under the bed and race toward a pile of clothes in the corner. Unwilling to admit defeat in front of his sons, Henry began to toss clothes from the pile into the middle of the floor. After a while, it was clear to all of them that the mouse was long gone.

Finally giving up, Henry loudly declared, "That rodent is dead! I'll get him boys! Anna, I'm going to the hardware store!" Henry called out to his wife, then stormed out of the house. A little later he returned with a box of rat poison, a small box of death held tightly in a brown paper bag.

Later that evening, a tiny mouse cautiously left his hole in the wall to start his nightly chores. His stomach rumbled and he caught an enticing scent. He followed the faint aroma to a little box underneath the kitchen sink. He took a deep whiff of the tempting cheese. The usual tantalizing smell had a stinging chemical note that burned his sensitive nose. If a scent could be sinister and cold, this was it. No matter how loud his stomach grumbled in protest, he knew he should run from this cheese.

The cupboard! He looked around quickly to be sure

the kitchen was clear. After the close call in the boys' bedroom, he knew he needed to be more careful about not being seen. Scampering nimbly up to the high cupboard, he nibbled on a small cracker and then scrambled through a crack in the door.

The tiny creature had watched the family's food supply shrink over the past few months. "How empty their stomachs must be!" Charlie wrote in his journal. "I know there must be something I can do to help. Tomorrow I'm going exploring to see what I can find. All is possible!"

Charlie tucked his journal into its special place,

settling into a little bed he'd made from a clump of cotton and a tiny box. He picked up his favorite book, *All is Possible*. The last words he read before he dozed off for the night were, "Do good things for others, this will bring you true happiness." Charlie decided to follow his heart as he fell into a deep sleep, dreaming of what he could do.

Words of Wisdom
Charlie's Favorite Quotes

If you find it in your heart to care for somebody else, you will have succeeded. – Maya Angelou

" There is a great difference between worry and concern. A worried person sees a problem, and a concerned person solves a problem." – Harold Stephens

I've learned that people will forget what you said, people will forget what you did, but people will never forget how you made them feel. – Maya Angelou

"Be the change that you want to see in the world" – Mohandas Gandhi

Chapter Four
Seeds of Inspiration

*"Happiness lies in the joy of achievement and the thrill
of creative effort."* –Franklin D. Roosevelt

The next day, Charlie went exploring in the most
tucked away places in the house. First, the attic;
Charlie figured he'd work from the top down. Every
inch, every closet, every drawer, Charlie inspected
it all. Nothing. Full of hope, he decided his next
stop would be the root cellar. But there he was
only greeted by a lot of old dust, dirt, cobwebs and
broken baskets.

As he evaluated all that was before him, the mouse
found something extraordinary. Way back in the far
corner of the root cellar he spotted a lone, wrinkled
potato. It was shriveled with age and sat beneath a
stream of light that offered enough life-giving energy
to produce two green, vibrant sprouts protruding
from one end.

Charlie moved slowly through the dust to inspect
the potato. The sprouts were healthy and eager to
live. They were reaching to the sky, in the direction
of the stream of light, and they quivered with life

when Charlie touched them. Looking past the sprouts Charlie saw a treasure trove of vegetables seeds bundled with a string just beyond the potato. Suddenly, it hit him!

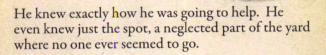

He knew just what to do.

He knew exactly how he was going to help. He even knew just the spot, a neglected part of the yard where no one ever seemed to go.

Looking up at the window, he started planning how to get these seed packets up to the yard. They weren't heavy, but they would still make for a hefty task for little Charlie. He looked around and saw a nice, fat stick. Carrying it back to the window, he put his little shoulder to the corner and shoved hard.

A small opening appeared and Charlie quickly pushed the stick as far into it as he could. Then, getting underneath the middle of the stick, he pushed with all his might. The window made a creaking noise and opened about two full inches! He scampered outside as fast as he could with the seeds in tow. He returned for the potato and carried it outside.

The earth outside was rock-hard, dry and lifeless from neglect. He tried scraping into the stony surface with one pointy sharp fingernail; just a tiny indent was visible. He looked at the tiny carrot seed he pulled from one of the packets. Charlie knew that if he placed it in the small indent, the roots would not be able to penetrate the hard soil. "How can I fix this? I can't think! I need some cheese!"

Charlie always thought better with a piece of cheese in his paws. He called it "Thinking Cheese." He would hold it, turn it over in his small paws, smell the sweet aroma of his favorite thing in the world and, when the time was just right, he would tilt his head back and drop the whole thing in his mouth. Thinking Cheese fulfilled its promise no matter how small the bit. It was like his ticket to all things possible, no matter how challenging the situation. Whenever he had a puzzle to solve or a solution to find, even the tiniest bit of cheese would do. It was like a magical potion that could turn every problem into an opportunity to create something spectacular!

This time, he searched his secret stash for a tasty morsel of scrumptiousness and genius. No luck! Unfazed, he nibbled on a fingernail, tasting the brown dust of the earth he'd tried to till. Not quite the yummy cheese his taste buds longed for, but at the moment he needed all the inspiration he could get. Looking around for the answer, he scoured every inch of the yard with his super-sharp, mouse vision until he discovered something.

What serendipity! What luck! Not far away, in a giant weed patch, he spotted something extremely useful! He scampered over to inspect a thatch of dry weeds. He scrambled along a dry rubber hose that lay like a slumbering snake in the grass, traveling its length until he came to an enormous pipe jutting from the ground, high into the air.

Then it occurred to Charlie that he was only four inches tall. The pipe must have been three feet high— nine times his height!

His eyes followed it. The pipe glimmered in the moonlight, beckoning him to its top as it loomed far above him.

He thought, "Once I get to the top of the pipe, will I be able to turn the handle? Can I do all this without anyone seeing me?"

Out of thinking cheese, he continued to nibble his fingernails instead. Such a nasty habit for Charlie! Taking a deep breath and standing tall, his determination grew.

"I can do it!" He looked carefully around the yard and up into the trees, not wanting to risk being seen by one of the family members or a hungry owl out for a midnight snack. No one in sight! He rubbed his tiny palms together briskly, adrenaline and energy pumping. He grasped the cool pipe and swiftly shimmied up the slick surface.

Now that he was at the top, Charlie's tiny hands grasped the enormous handle. He tugged and pulled, shifted and pushed until he felt the smallest of movements! Was that enough? Better try harder! With one more firm tug, using every bit of strength he possessed, the handle gave way!

Charlie was ecstatic to feel the water coursing through the hose. He scrambled down the pipe, once again following the hose to where the cool water ran like a rushing river quenching the thirst of the hard, dry ground. Charlie looked on contently. "I knew it was possible! All is possible!" he thought, jumping up and down.

Charlie tended his field well, shifting the hose until each bit of ground had gotten a deep drink. He then ran back to turn off the hose. The ground was ready for the tiny seedlings.

Charlie dug a small hole and rolled the potato into its new home, partially covering it with dirt. Using an old roofing nail to plow straight furrows, Charlie masterfully dropped the seeds into the tiny holes, planting something new each night. Before long, the hard part was done. He slapped his hands together, knocking off the last of the soil. The mouse looked up to survey the work he'd done thus far and imagined his lovely garden. It's going to be beautiful!

Now I'll just have to keep the garden watered and battle an occasional predator, like a snail or slug, he thought, determined. Soon the seeds will grow into tiny green shoots. There will be bush beans, potatoes, lettuce, tomatoes, carrots, squash, garlic, onions and tender herbs. He took a deep breath and rocked back and forth on his feet in deep satisfaction. He could almost see Anna's pretty face hovering over a pot, taking in the tantalizing aroma as the vegetables simmered on the stove.

Little did Charlie know, there was someone watching him hard at work.

CHAPTER FIVE
A SECRET GARDENER

"Little things have the power to enrich our lives; they can change our hearts, our perspectives and our attitudes."
-Author unknown

After all was quiet each night, Anna darned and patched the many worn and tired socks. Henry sat by the kitchen window, silent, sometimes sighing, always worrying. He listened to radio reports of growing food shortages, longer bread lines and fights that would break out in the cities.

One night, while blankly staring out of the window, a flicker of movement caught Henry's attention.

"What's that?" Henry squinted, unsuccessfully trying to make out a shape in the darkness. Henry curiously watched each night for weeks. The movement he had noticed always seemed to be in the midst of the new plants that recently began to pop up amidst the weeds. He also noticed that someone was taking great care to water and weed the area. Some mornings, he noticed tiny footprints in the mud. This little patch of dirt seemed determined to grow something. "Probably just more weeds!" Henry mumbled gruffly.

The weeks leading up to the first ripe vegetables in Charlie's garden were the most difficult for the family. Meat was scarce. Fruit was not to be found. Butter was long gone. Even the drippings they'd used to moisten bread were gone. They lived off eggs, cheese and beans. Each week, the meager rations they could afford got smaller. This situation had forced the entire family to take on odd jobs, even the youngest sold newspapers to bring in extra money. Henry feared he would soon give in to hopelessness.

Yet, hope was not lost to everyone. Each night after dark, the little mouse had painstakingly prepared the soil, digging and scraping with a small shard of broken pottery. The area for the garden was enormous for a mouse his size. But Charlie was determined! He envisioned the day when the lush, tasty veggies from the garden would fill the tummies of Henry's family.

The garden was big for little Charlie—but he realized it wouldn't be long before he could have this land ready. He told himself, "If I work one area at a time, I can do it." He poked and prodded, working first one section and then the next. On nights with a bright bold moon, Charlie was especially cautious, not wanting to be discovered by the neighbor's cat, Chester. On dark, moonless nights, he was thankful that his sharp mouse vision allowed him to work under the cover of darkness. His keen sense of smell alerted him when Chester or another danger was nearby. Night after night, Charlie worked the ground until his tiny paws were sore.

Henry's family was down to one stale piece of bread. It had been left on a plate on the kitchen table. It sat, almost trophy-like, for days. It was one of the last scraps of food in the kitchen. The whole family wanted it. Henry and his wife thought they should save it for the boys. But Henry's young sons, aware of their family's dire straits, had secretly agreed to keep it for the person in the family who might need it the most. And as Andy was prone to late night snacks, Richard threatened to hogtie him if he broke that promise! Even with the threat, Richard still kept a close eye on him.

Strangely, if one examined the bread closely, there were small nibble marks along the edges. Henry and his wife had noticed them and wondered  which one of their kids was being so tentative about eating it. Day after day, as the nibble marks increased, Henry looked at the piece of bread with growing despair, a vivid reminder of the grimness of his family's situation. It was a sad reminder of how dire their situation had become. It also served as a rallying cry for him every time he went out to look for work. All of their efforts only seemed to delay the inevitable. The last piece of bread had to go someday.

Henry came home disappointed again from a long day's job search to see the mouse dart across the kitchen with a big piece of the stale bread in his mouth. He snapped! In an instant he ripped off one of his tattered work boots and was about to throw it at the mouse with everything he had. At that precise moment, Charlie turned to look at Henry with a mouthful of food.

Henry saw a gleam in the mouse's eyes. It was just a flicker that told of going to bed night after night clutching his growling stomach, just like Henry's own family.

This was the same mouse Henry had seen working in the yard at night. He realized that the small mouse was only after something to eat and a place to stay. In fact, the mouse had actually been earning his keep in the yard. The mouse was only looking to survive like everyone else. Henry's heart would not allow him to throw the boot.

Charlie realized his life was being spared and bolted to the safety of his home in the wall. Sighing heavily, Henry allowed the boot to drop to the floor beside his leg. For a few moments, he stared at the spot on the floor where the mouse had been, thankful for the pause that gave the mouse a chance to escape. He wasn't a cruel man. He knew he would've regretted harming a helpless mouse.

As he did so, he noticed a trail of tiny footprints just like the ones he'd seen in the garden. He bent lower to take a closer look, rubbing his eyes just to be sure. Now he really began to wonder what was going on in his own backyard when, suddenly, he noticed the time and realized he was almost late. He stripped off his other boot, put both his shoes away and walked quickly into the living room. Then he sank into his comfy armchair with a big, relaxing sigh.

He leaned over and gently tuned his small Philips radio to the President's latest fireside chat. Franklin D. Roosevelt was a personal hero of his and he found great comfort in hearing the President's voice over the crackling airwaves. Hearing the radio, Anna and the kids joined Henry, huddling close together. They all held hands for the next 35 minutes as they listened intently to the voice of their president.

After the broadcast, as Anna and Henry were preparing for bed, Anna saw Henry write the word "boondoggle" on a slip of paper. "If we can boondoggle ourselves out of this depression, that word is going to be enshrined in the hearts of the American people for years to come," Roosevelt had said. Anna smiled, remembering the President's voice in her head as she watched her husband slip the paper under his pillow. He looked up at her and bashfully confessed, "Just something to sleep on ... for inspiration."

The following morning, our clever little gardener, who had learned so much during his time with the family, practiced his writing skills. He took his tiny pencil and wrote a small note for Henry. Strategically placing the note on the table where Henry would be sure to find it, Charlie left a perfectly ripe tomato from the garden on top of the note.

When Henry awoke, he walked quietly into the kitchen so as not to wake the rest of the family. To his surprise he found a bright red tomato sitting quaintly on the kitchen table. He glanced around, wondering where it could've come from. Seeing nothing out of the ordinary, he picked up the tomato and lightly stroked the smooth crimson skin. He was surprised to find the accompanying note and fumbled for his reading glasses.

Thank you for sparing my life, sir. You will not regret it!

Henry was completely flabbergasted by the note.

"What is this?! Did the boys do this? Do they think they're clever, stamping a tiny paw print on it?" He woke them up, demanding answers from them, but they swore it wasn't their doing. Trying to piece everything together, he ran outside with the note. His family remained inside watching bewildered through the window.

Henry took a look around the garden, amazed at the bountiful produce. Dangling from tall vines, instead of growing wild on the ground, were neat rows of long green pods. If he didn't know any better, they might have been green beans. He continued to let his eyes wander and saw the small, hard globes of tomatoes just beginning to turn red. Then, there were full heads of lettuce growing like big beautiful green roses. Next to them, the cabbages nestled tightly in their broad, grey leaves, all of them organized in a neat little grid. At the end, corn stalks were rising upwards to meet the sun. As his eyes trailed downwards, he noticed his most important discovery of all — there were more tiny footprints like he'd seen from the note.

Gasping in surprise, Henry put the pieces together, mumbling to himself, "As impossible as it seems, this mouse is our little gardener!" He scratched his head, not even believing himself as he said it.

Filled with awe, Henry surveyed the garden. He reflected on the courage and determination it took for a tiny mouse to plant such an incredible amount of food. There was enough to feed Henry's whole family. It must have taken the mouse months with all his strength every day to plant a thousand times his capacity. Charlie's kindness and hard work humbled Henry.

But even more extraordinary, Henry thought, "Why would the mouse do this for my family after I tried to get rid of him?" He thought back to the box of rat poison he had purchased, filled with remorse. Henry read the note several times and each time felt a growing amazement at the unselfish act of kindness.

Staring at a backyard blooming with food, Henry's

heart felt lighter and more carefree than it had in a very long time. He realized that there were grand lessons to be learned, even from a creature as small as a mouse. Seeing such unconditional kindness reinspired his passion for life, he suddenly felt the overwhelming desire to show others the same kindness the mouse had shown him.

CHAPTER SIX
OPPORTUNITIES EVERYWHERE

*"We shall not fail or falter; we shall not weaken or tire...
Give us the tools and we shall finish the job."*
– Franklin D. Roosevelt

Henry started the next day with an overwhelming sense of gratitude. He looked at the houses on his block and realized he could take his carpentry skills to help the neighborhood. Everywhere he looked he saw dilapidated homes. The mouse had done a very nice thing for his family when he had planted the seeds. Now it was as if Henry was looking with new eyes and it suddenly seemed opportunities were visible everywhere!

Overwhelmed with eagerness, Henry called to his boys. Sensing the refreshing excitement in his voice, they ran outside and huddled around their father, nodding with approval as they heard Henry's plan. They all set out with a borrowed wheelbarrow and an air of determination. Hours later, they returned from the dump on the edge of town, their wheelbarrow brimming with building materials that looked remotely useable.

The first house they visited was Mrs. Roberts' on

the corner. "Whatcha want?" she called out, fearful that they were going to complain about the state of her yard. She knew what everyone was saying. And she was embarrassed. But she was an old lady with children who were scattered to the four winds. She was alone, had very little money and just couldn't do it on her own.

"Mrs. Roberts, we've come to help you get your place fixed up," Henry said with a smile. The old woman looked at him as though he'd said something crazy.

"Whatcha mean you're gonna help me fix up my place?" she said. "I know you're out of work Henry. I can't pay you. I've got no money or I'd have got this place fixed myself, long ago. I'm sorry. I can't hire you."

"Not lookin' to get hired, ma'am. Just lookin' to get your house in order for you. My boys and I have the time. May take us a bit, but you give us permission and we'll do the work." In astonishment, Mrs. Roberts could not say anything else.

Henry and the boys patched the stairs and straightened the post, taking extra care to make it sturdy and safe. With that little bit of work, Mrs. Roberts' place looked better already. She was so pleased by their kindness that her grumpy demeanor melted a bit. Henry thought he might have seen the wrinkled corners of her mouth turn up slightly, a faint light of hope in her eyes.

"Boys, wait here," Mrs. Roberts called out and then disappeared into the house.

"Here, take these. My sister brought me a couple of baskets of apples. I can't use them all. You take one," Mrs. Roberts said, handing the basket to one of the boys, Richard.

"Thank you so very much ma'am. We're truly grateful." Henry tipped his worn hat. Andy and Richard nodded their thanks. The boys took turns pushing the wheelbarrow back home, each munching on a crisp, juicy apple along the way.

"I can't wait 'til Mom sees these!" Andy said, with a mouth full of tart green apple.

The next day, Henry and the boys went to the Ferguson's home to see how they might help. First, they fixed a squeaky old door with a bit of grease and some paint. Then they patched a hole in the floor so Mr. Ferguson wouldn't break his ankle. Finally, they wrenched a drippy water faucet into dry submission. Beaming, Mr. Ferguson gave Henry and the boys a large bag of rice and a few bags of beans for their trouble. The three of them returned home deeply fulfilled from their hard day's work, silently hoping they'd be able to find more ways to help the next day.

Words of Wisdom
Charlie's Favorite Quotes

"Three helping one another will do as much as six men singly." – Spanish Proverb

"In helping others, we shall help ourselves, for whatever good we give out completes the circle and comes back to us." – Flora Edwards

"Happiness never decreases by being shared." –Buddha

"Wherever a man turns he can find someone who needs him." – Albert Schweitzer

"In about the same degree as you are helpful, you will be happy." – Karl Reiland

"A good heart is better than all the heads in the world." – Edward Bulwer-Lytton

"To care for anyone else enough to make their problems one's own, is ever the beginning of one's real development." – Felix Adler

"Once you've had a taste of serving, you won't be able to leave it. Because there is joy in serving others." – Swami Kriyananda

"You give little when you give of your possessions; it is when you give of yourself that you truly give." – Khalil Gibran

CHAPTER SEVEN
PART OF THE FAMILY

"The test of our progress is not whether we add more to the abundance of those who have much; it is whether we provide enough for those who have too little."
– Franklin D. Roosevelt

By the end of the second day, the wheelbarrow was empty. The next day Henry and the kids went back to the garbage dump for more material. There were more houses to fix. The word had spread about what the family was doing. While Henry and the kids were out replenishing their supplies, Anna was home taking work orders from dozens of people.

All of their neighbors had something to offer in appreciation for the work, mostly food and clothes. One woman offered her sewing skills, another man offered to tutor the kids. After a week, Grandpa Henry's kitchen was filled with food, and the kids had new outfits and games to boot.

Each day, they found a new way to help a neighbor. Each day, new hope came to the community and the neighbors grew a little friendlier. Each day, Henry and his family were more and more grateful for the bounty provided by Charlie's garden. They shared it with the neighbors, completely changing the spirit of the neighborhood. Even grumpy Mrs. Roberts would wave to the boys as they passed by.

Richard told the family about Mrs. Roberts. "Yesterday, I saw a different Mrs. Roberts. She smiled at me warmly, for the first time, and said 'You boys have fixed much more than just my porch.'" Anna brightly said, "You guys are my heroes." And then Andy enthusiastically shared how Mr. Ferguson said, "Your father's genuine kindness started something in our community and it's contagious. Your generous actions have brought hope where there was none before. Thank you."

Anna looked proudly at Henry. Henry's face softened and it looked like tears began gathering in the corners of his eyes. He looked at the cupboard; it was full of food. There was a new kind of warmth and invigorating energy in his family and, now, the whole neighborhood.

Henry was filled with emotion. "The mouse is the real hero," he said. The rest of the family nodded in agreement. Anna looked around the table and said, "Maybe we can do something for him." Andy excitedly suggested, "It seems like he loves food and he's given us so much already. Maybe we can invite him to dinner." "Great, let's do it!" Henry agreed. Anna said, "I can make the mouse a pair of tiny overalls to wear proudly while he tends the garden and a little suit just in case he wants to dress up sometimes."

Then the table was silent for a moment, as if everyone was reflecting on how amazing the mouse was. Anna was the first to break the silence. "He has such a big heart," she said softly. "He's the King of Hearts," Richard excitedly added. Henry suggested, "Let's call him Charlie." The family looked at him curiously.

Henry explained, "Each king in a deck of playing cards represents a great king from history:

> Spades - King David
> Clubs - Alexander, the Great
> Diamonds - Julius Caesar
> Hearts - Charlemagne

King Charlemagne was also known as Charles the Great. He lived in the 8th century. He was considered the father of Europe, and his empire united most of Western Europe for the first time since the Romans."

"Wow, how do you know that, Dad?" Andy exclaimed. Henry shrugged and told his boys, "I still remember a thing or two from my schoolboy days.

I love history, it's so important to learn from our past so we can make better decisions for our future. "

Now, it was Henry's turn to write a note. Along with the new clothes, he left the message on the floor next to the refrigerator with a chunk of Swiss cheese.

Mouse,
Your generous act of kindness has not only changed our family, but our whole community. It's extraordinary and inspiring what one compassionate individual can do.

We'd like you to be our guest of honor. Please meet us in the kitchen at 6pm for dinner. If mice can't tell time, follow your nose to the smell of vegetables, rice and bean soup. Anna and the boys are expecting you. Me too. And by the way we gave you the name Charlie. Hope that works for you.

-Henry

Charlie arrived right on time. He wore the neatly pressed navy blue suit Anna had made for him. In his lapel was a perfect thyme blossom. He gave a little bow as he greeted his hosts.

"Good evening, Charlie. Dinner is ready. We're so happy to have you with us," Anna said. Charlie could smell the tantalizing aroma of Anna's soup and feel the warmth emanating from the gazes of everyone at the table. He was so excited! He'd always dreamt of being accepted by them and here he was, the guest of honor at a family dinner. He was so overwhelmed all he could do was stand there, breathless.

"Well, look at you! I see you understood my note. I didn't believe it at first but you are quite an exceptional mouse! Charlie, we've got just the spot for you," Henry said as he reached down with his outstretched palm to offer Charlie a ride to the table. Charlie stepped onto Henry's palm and was escorted to the place of honor.

"I made this table just for you," Richard said proudly as Henry gently placed Charlie next to a miniature table. Anna donated a crocheted doily as a colorful rug and a sliver of fabric as padding for his tiny chair. Andy set it all up on top of the kitchen table. The family sat down all together, ready to eat.

"Here you are Charlie," Anna said. She dished a

healthy helping of soup into a small egg cup. Charlie admired the feast on the table. There was piping hot soup, a salad made from fresh red tomatoes, tender lettuce, crisp cucumbers and sliced sweet carrots all picked that very morning.

The family watched this magical creature silently pantomiming his appreciation. Without a single spoken word, they knew exactly what Charlie was experiencing as he took in the sights and smells of this amazing dinner. The soup sat piping hot, its steam carrying the luscious aroma up to his whiskered nose. He closed his eyes and paused for a minute, savoring each scent, waving the fragrant steam in the direction of his tiny twitching nose with his miniature paw. Pungent sweet onions, glorious garlic, zucchini, rich tomatoes! Wait there's something more! He pondered what it might be. One more tiny distinguishing whiff and he had it. Ahh yes! It's the thyme and rosemary! Lovely!

Charlie picked up the perfectly pressed mouse-sized napkin Anna had made for him, gave it a firm shake to unfold it and tucked it into his shirt collar. Now it's time to taste! He picked up the spoon Richard had carved for him from some of the leftover wood from his table project. He dipped it carefully in the steamy broth, testing it against his tongue. A burned tongue would rob him of savoring the intricate flavors of this feast! It was perfect. He took a sip of the flavorful broth then scooped up the vegetables, rice and beans. At first the family barely spoke, not wanting to interrupt Charlie's extreme enjoyment of the meal, nor wanting to miss every changing blissful expression that passed across his face.

Finally Henry spoke, "Anna, I don't think I've ever seen anyone enjoy a meal quite like Charlie here. I think we might learn a bit from this mouse." The whole family nodded and smiled in full agreement with Henry.

Charlie took a long drink of cool milk from a thimble. He looked up from his delirium and flashed a smile. A milk mustache coated his upper lip and whiskers. The smile was so broad, so charming, the family broke into a chorus of laughter.  Charlie joined them in their merriness and his tiny squeaks of laughter were the first sounds they'd heard Charlie utter. The meal continued with warm conversation. It was truly a meal to remember for all of them, a time of celebration and renewed hope.

The family's home repair business, Happy Houses, began all those years ago. By the time Sandy came along, the family was successfully swimming in money and tales of hungry nights were merely legends. All of it was due to Charlie the mouse getting caught with a mouthful of stolen bread and Great Grandpa Henry's sympathetic heart. From that day on, Charlie was a cherished part of the family.

CHAPTER EIGHT
A MYSTERIOUS JOURNAL

"Learn from the mistakes of others.
You can't live long enough to make them all yourself."
-Eleanor Roosevelt

Exasperated, Mitch checked his phone for messages. No calls, no messages, no emails—no job!

"How long can we go on like this?" he sighed deeply.

In an attempt to distract himself from all of these worries, Mitch decided to worry about dinner instead. He began looking through the cupboards for ideas. Out of the corner of his eye, in a spot he had never really looked in before, he saw the ragged corner of a very small book. It was about the size of a business card and about one inch thick. He reached back into the corner and pulled out an old leather-bound journal.

He gently lifted the cover of the worn journal and was surprised to see tiny handwritten notes in curly script, some accompanied by meticulous drawings. He could barely read the script, but stepping back into the light and focusing carefully, he could make

Carrot Loaf

1 cup ground raw carrots
1 cup boiled rice
1 cup ground peanuts
1 egg
4 tbsp. minced red
    or green peppers
2 tbsp. butter
5 tbsp. minced onions
1 tsp. mustard
Salt and pepper

Mix ingredients in order
and bake the loaf on
moderate heat for 1 hour.
Serve with tomato sauce
if desired or Golden
Opportunity Sauce.

Golden Opportunity Sauce

1 cup potatoes,
    cooked
1 cup carrots, cooked
1 - 2 cups water
(reserve and use liquid from
cooking the potatoes and
carrots)
1 tbsp. Bragg's liquid
aminos (or soy sauce)
1 tbsp. fresh lemon juice
1 - 2 garlic cloves, pressed

Using a blender, add all
ingredients and process
until desired smoothness.
Heat and serve over
Carrot Loaf.

out a collection of thoughts, quotes, ramblings and recipes. One recipe in particular caught Mitch's attention. "This one sounds easy. I'll try it," he decided. Mitch had the table set when Sandy got home from work.

"This looks good," said Sandy, taking her place at the table and excited for the prospect of a pleasant dinner together. "Have you made this before?" The dish reminded her of a dish her Grandmother used to make when she was a child.

"It's new," Mitch replied. "I found the recipe in this old book today. It must have been left by the previous renters."

Sandy hid her surprise when she saw the very familiar journal. It was Charlie's! Sandy wondered if this might be a good time to tell Mitch about Charlie. She decided against it, knowing that it would be quite a shock for Mitch and not wanting to ruin a lovely dinner.

"This is delicious, Mitch. Thank you so much for making it. It's nice to come home and have dinner with you like this," Sandy said, quickly changing the subject. She was enjoying the meal too much to add conflict to the menu.

The next morning, out of curiosity, Mitch spent a few minutes leafing through the dry, brittle pages of the old journal. He wondered at the skill it would take to write such tiny, neat letters. Some of the more recent notes were tacked in or written on sticky notes. Coincidentally, just like that first note he found in the house. There was so much here! The entries that began in the '30s, continued through World War II into the '60s and to the present day in the new millennium. There was so much going on that Mitch found it hard to absorb it all. But he did notice that a common thread of all the entries was kindness and service to others, especially when times were tough.

Another common theme was food. The writer seemed to be absolutely in love with food in all respects—eating, cooking and gardening. There were detailed notes and information about gardening like when and where to plant different vegetables. The notes were accompanied by detailed drawings of different recipes, vegetables and fruits. A section titled, "Foods: Pure and Simple" caught Mitch's attention.

As Mitch continued to read the entries, he grew more and more puzzled. He had an uncanny feeling when he realized that many of the names in the book were very familiar ones, like 'Andy.' Sandy's dad's name is Andrew. Her grandpa was Andy. While curious, Mitch couldn't make heads or tails of his findings and thus decided it must only be coincidence. He was delighted to find another perfect recipe that would surprise Sandy for the second night in a row. Having grown tired of spaghetti or hamburgers for every meal, and recalling the satisfaction of cooking a meal for Sandy the night before, Mitch was excited to try his hand at what seemed like a delicious vegetable recipe.

Creamy Cheesy Spinach Casserole

2 lbs. of spinach
1 cup parmesan or other grated cheese
2 tbsp. butter
1 cup onions

Wash spinach, add water, cook over medium heat for about 6 to 8 minutes. Drain, add all ingredients except bread crumbs. Pour into approximately 10" x 6" baking dish. Top with bread crumbs. Bake at 450° for 12 to 15 minutes. Sprinkle nuts of your choice on top.

Speaking of food, Mitch took a break to get a quick snack from the kitchen. "I had muenster in here yesterday! Where did it go?" he mumbled. He discovered a few crackers with telltale nibble marks on them. "Ugh! Rodents!" he said to himself mindlessly.

Mitch grudgingly settled for an apple instead and then retreated back to his location on the living room couch.

He thought back to the recipe he would prepare for dinner that night and to the other recipes in the fragile yellowed pages of the small journal. The recipes all sounded surprisingly good. They were certainly not very gourmet or sophisticated like the ones he'd seen on the cable food channel but they looked tasty, easy to make and were unexpectedly economical. One recipe in particular caught his eye.

Just then, Mitch's neglected cell phone uttered a shriek from the kitchen table. Running over to pick it up, he fought off a faint twinge of hope for an employer. After a brief conversation, Mitch was

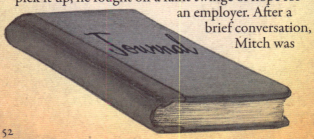

delighted to find out that he had been scheduled for an interview the next day at 10 am.

With a new sense of optimism, Mitch left for the store to get the missing muenster cheese and the other ingredients he needed for tonight's celebratory dinner. He briefly thought about the fact that for the first time in his life, he wasn't spending a lot of time thinking and worrying about how much he was spending. It wasn't as tough as he thought it would be.

"What else do I need?" Mitch thought, "Oh yes, rodent traps and a bottle of wine to celebrate!"

When Mitch got home, he set two of the rodent traps, one behind the stove and the other under the sink. Then he enthusiastically began preparing the special dinner from the recipe, hoping that it would delight and surprise Sandy just as the night before.

That night's dinner was even more scrumptious than that of the night before. Sandy was again

53

delighted with Mitch's gesture and listened intently as he tried to contain his excitement for his interview the next day. He talked tirelessly about what he hoped to get out of the interview.

"Oh, Sandy, I'm nervous. But you know, I'm also really excited for tomorrow. This could mean everything for us. It could be our opportunity to buy a stunning house in an upscale neighborhood again. We'll be back to where we were. No, we'll be even better off than we were before and I'll work harder than ever this time."

Trying to hide her disappointment, Sandy just smiled to be supportive. When Mitch suggested a toast to a better life, she lifted her wine glass, but her heart was not in it. The things Mitch described were not in the better life that she had dreamed of for the two of them. Feeling scared and not knowing how to react to Mitch's enthusiasm, she could only think about Charlie. She tried to imagine what he would do in this situation. She almost decided to tell Mitch right then and there about Charlie. But like the night before, the fear that he would not understand overpowered her and she put it off again. "Oh, this isn't the right time to tell him about Charlie. I need to let him focus on his interview," Sandy thought sadly. They clinked their glasses together and Sandy offered a weak smile. "You'll do an amazing job tomorrow, Mitch."

CHAPTER NINE
WORST DAY EVER!

"Sometimes good things fall apart so better things can fall together." –Marilyn Monroe

That night, Mitch could barely sleep, he was so excited for his interview the next morning. He got up from bed early and saw Sandy off to work. After she left, he checked the mousetraps he had set the day before. He was surprised to find that neither of the traps were where he had left them. Mitch stood perplexed, looking at the empty spaces.

Breaking out of his daze and realizing that if he didn't get going soon, he would be late for his interview, Mitch picked up the garbage and headed out the door. The door closed behind him with a bang. Suddenly, he panicked. He stopped dead in his tracks as he felt his pockets. Smacking his forehead, Mitch was terrified to realize that he had forgotten his keys inside the house. Sandy was not home, and none of the other doors or windows were likely to be open. Realizing it was futile, Mitch banged on the door anyway and tried calling Sandy's name out of desperation. He violently twisted the doorknob, hoping he could just will it to be open. No luck.

The commotion shook little Charlie, tucked away in his hole inside the house. Curious, he peeked out and looked at the door. Mitch's silhouette greeted him from the window. Wondering what could be wrong, Charlie scanned the kitchen and noticed Mitch's keys lying on the table, sunlight reflecting off of them. Now he knew what was wrong.

Jumping into action, Charlie rushed over to the stand next to the door where dirty shoes and backyard tools were stored. He nimbly scampered to the top of the stand until he was able to reach the doorknob. He threw his body onto the knob and began to kick his legs forward. The knob turned a bit, but then he lost his footing and tumbled to the floor.

Undeterred, and determined to help Mitch, Charlie climbed back onto the stand and repositioned himself on the doorknob again. He began to push. As soon as he felt the knob turning, he lost his footing once more and tumbled down.

Charlie rose slowly, confused. He had thought that he would be able to open the door for Mitch that time. But he was doing something not quite right.

If he only knew what it was. Charlie had seen people open doors before, lots of times. They walked up, turned the doorknob and it opened. Why was this not working for him? He struggled to remain calm as he tried to figure out how to open the door. Meanwhile, Mitch had been pacing back and forth by the door, worried and anxious about getting to his interview. He realized that he had also left his phone inside, so he couldn't even call the potential employer to let him know he might be late. He tried the front door again, knowing that it would not open. He tried the back door again, almost knocking Charlie off the doorknob.

For a moment, Mitch thought he saw a little gray mouse on the doorknob through the window. But he dismissed the idea, sighing, "I must be losing it."

Charlie decided to try his luck with the doorknob one more time. He once again wrapped his body around the knob. This time, instead of pushing his feet from the stand, he repositioned himself sideways and began to push from the wall as he turned the knob.

Outside, Mitch sat down on the back porch overwhelmed with frustration and anxiety. With his elbows on his knees he sighed, "I can't believe this is happening to me." In a last futile attempt, he called out Sandy's name.

Just then, Charlie lost his grip on the knob and tumbled to the floor with a small thump. To his delight, the door uttered a slight creak and opened just a fraction of an inch. Ecstatic, Charlie did flips in the air.

Mitch heard the small thumping noise of the little mouse falling to the floor and the creaking of the door as it opened. He curiously pushed the door open. He couldn't believe it! It opened! This was a miracle! He looked around the kitchen but found no one there. He didn't notice the little mouse watching happily from his hiding place.

Realizing that he was already 20 minutes late for his interview, Mitch dismissed the miracle, grabbed his keys from the kitchen table and rushed out the door. He hoped that he would still be able to speak to the employer and was more and more nervous every minute. When he arrived, his heart sank. There were already several people waiting in the office for an interview. He was one of many who were applying for the same position. Nervous, but still hopeful, he sat down and began chatting with the others. To his continued dismay, they were all not only more qualified than he was, but had been out of work much longer. They were desperate and were willing to accept a salary far less than what he had been used to. His hopes were shattered.

Meanwhile, back at home, Charlie was looking for a tasty way to celebrate his victory. He looked through the refrigerator for a delicious treat. Suddenly, he caught a sharp, tangy, sweet scent with his small nose. His mouth instantly began watering and he searched for the source of the delightful smell. He began his quest in the bins at the bottom and then skillfully climbed up the wire shelving, twirling and swinging from shelf to shelf like a trapeze artist.

At last, he found just what he was looking for on the top shelf—key lime pie, a personal favorite! Charlie stood at the side of the pie plate and quickly found the cool creamy topping. He scooped up a pawful of the tasty treat and put it to his mouth, drawn in by its syrupy, slippery goodness! He slid into the sweet, tart filling, virtually swimming in the frothy cream. He took big gulps, smacking his lips and licking each finger clean. Charlie was floating on a creamy cloud, feeling like he was in key lime heaven.

Charlie was completely covered in the sweet, tart filling. Pie ran down the entire front of his body. After finishing his treat, he would have to clean himself. Never had his fingers and toes tasted so good! Charlie's sweet tooth was finally satisfied. Feeling perfectly content from the sugar rush, he tumbled back over the side of the tin and slipped out of the fridge, carelessly leaving a tiny trail of untidy footprints. He returned to his small hole, sticky but satisfied and took a quick sponge bath to remove the sticky, yummy goo. The sugar gave Charlie a short-lived rush followed by an irresistible urge for a nap. He woke up hours later to the sound of Mitch yelling.

Crushed by his unfortunate day and even more unfortunate interview, Mitch arrived at home determined to drown his sorrow by digging into the last slice of one of his favorite treats—key lime pie. It had been on his mind the whole drive home. "At least that's something I can look forward to," he muttered to himself as he opened the refrigerator door.

It was not uncommon for Mitch to crave something sweet when he was really frustrated. It gave him a little emotional pick-me-up.

"Key lime pie! Here I come!" Mitch playfully called

out as he opened the fridge. Instead of his picture perfect pie, he found a completely scrambled mess and a trail of sticky prints leading away from the fridge. Furious, he yelled, "How could a rodent get into a refrigerator, climb up three shelves and paddle through my favorite dessert? This is just what I needed! Why my pie when there's plenty of other food in this kitchen?!" Mitch grumbled gruffly.

Still grumpy about the key lime pie incident, Mitch tried to distract himself by cleaning up the dishes from the night before. He slipped his antique wedding ring from his finger, placed it on the side of the sink and plunged his hands into the warm soapy water. The warm silky water soothed his frazzled spirit. As he scrubbed the dishes, he thought over the past few years.

"How did I get here? Why?! Sandy and I had everything! Now what have we got?" Mitch scooped the silverware from the counter into the sink with a clatter. As he rinsed the last of the utensils, he pulled the plug and watched the swirling water sweep into the drain, his energy draining along with it. Turning to put the ring back on his finger, he realized that it was missing.

"No! No! No!" Mitch yelled. This was the last straw.

Charlie, hearing Mitch's cries, scampered quickly into the kitchen. Mitch was kneeling under the sink, a wrench in his hand unscrewing the U-shaped pipe. He looked inside it and turned it over just to be sure he didn't miss anything. "She's going to kill me! She's going to KILL me!" he repeatedly muttered as he searched. "I knew I shouldn't have taken that ring off!" Mitch dug his fingers into the pipe as the dripping water formed a small puddle on the floor.

"Not a good day! First I get locked out, late to a

disastrous interview, then the RAT in the pie. Now this!" Mitch groaned. He threw the wrench down in frustration and stormed out of the room.

Charlie remembered the rings Mitch and Sandy wore on their left hands. Humans called them wedding rings and these were extra special. Sandy gave Great Grandpa Henry's wedding band to Mitch as a symbol of their love. It had been passed down the family, in homage to Henry and Anna. Had Mitch lost the ring?

Charlie had often followed the maze of pipes during his explorations of the cottage. He knew what he had to do to help Mitch. Not wasting any time, he ran to the sink as fast as he could before Mitch returned to the room. Then he shimmied into the narrow pipe and began making his way in the dark. He used his heightened senses to the best of his ability, but he still had to move slowly on his search for Mitch's ring. The pipes were damp and slippery and the ring had already traveled a long way. His whiskers helped him sense the turns in the pipes and he squinted to see as far ahead as he could. He searched and searched, unwilling to give up because he knew how much that ring meant to Sandy.

Hours later, Charlie emerged victorious from the plumbing maze, covered in slimy, smelly muck. Locked between Charlie's teeth was the precious wedding band. It, too, was covered in filth, but nothing a little soap and water couldn't fix. Charlie looked for signs of Mitch. The coast was clear so he quickly scrambled up to the kitchen sink, knocked over the dish detergent and began to lather up with the thick blue liquid. He scrubbed himself from head to tail and cleaned the ring thoroughly before jumping into a bowl of water for a quick rinse. He picked up the ring in his teeth once again and hopped to the top of the drain board ready to scramble back toward his home.

The adventure through the pipes had left Charlie feeling ravenous! His pointed nose caught wind of an inviting pungent aroma. Following the scent, he discovered a note from his dear friend, Sandy:

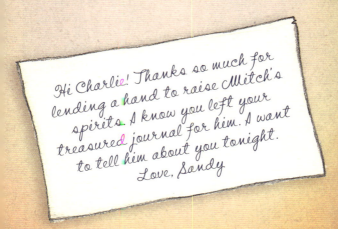

Hi Charlie! Thanks so much for lending a hand to raise Mitch's spirits. I know you left your treasured journal for him. I want to tell him about you tonight.
Love, Sandy

Charlie nibbled on the cheese as he read the note, then he ran home. Once there, he tucked the remaining cheese away in a little niche in the wall, saving it for a late night snack or early breakfast treat. Then Charlie, slipping a bit of Thinking Cheese into his pocket, got out his tiny pencil and sticky notes. He chewed thoughtfully on the end of the pencil thinking over what to write. Charlie scribbled for a bit and tucked the note away for later. After all that, he dropped exhausted onto his warm comfy bed, yawned and fell fast asleep. "I'll give this to Mitch after a little na...." He was out!

Bean and Kale Scramble

1 medium onion
1 cup beans, cooked
2 tsp. of dried Italian
    seasoning
2 cups kale, chopped
2 eggs

1 tbsp. lemon juice, fresh
2 tbsp. water
1 tbsp. Bragg's liquid aminos
  (or soy sauce)
2 cloves garlic, pressed

Sauté the onion in water till soft, 3 minutes.
Add the beans and seasoning and cook 3 more
minutes. Add the the remaining ingredients and
sauté for 5 minutes, stirring occasionally.

Chapter Ten
Charlie, Where Are You?!

"Our truest life is when we are in dreams awake."
–Henry David Thoreau

That night, Mitch was in a terrible mood. Just before Sandy arrived, he had set down the last two mouse traps, in hopes that this time they would get the pie thief. When Sandy got home, he had dinner ready, another delicious recipe from the mysterious journal.

When Sandy saw the dinner, all perfectly laid out on the kitchen table, she thanked Mitch for the lovely meal. "You did it again. Something completely new! Are all these recipes from that journal?" she asked, secretly knowing the source. She smiled to herself, thinking it was the perfect night to finally tell Mitch about Charlie.

"They are indeed from that journal I've been reading," Mitch replied, slumping into his chair at the table.

Sandy noticed his foul mood and realized his day had probably gone badly. She sat down with him and gently asked how his interview had gone.

Mousse in a Minute

6 ripe bananas, cut
1 cup applesauce
2 tbsp. carob powder
(may substitute cocoa powder)
1 tsp. vanilla or mint
(use fresh mint if available)

Blend all ingredients in
food processor till smooth.
Thickens upon refrigeration.
Serve chilled.

"To tell you the truth, it was awful. I've never felt so discouraged in my life. There were others there who were more qualified, had been unemployed for over a year and were willing to accept a salary that was insulting," Mitch sighed.

Sandy wished she knew how to tell him that it had probably happened for a reason, and that an even better opportunity was probably right around the corner. She knew he didn't want to hear it, but it had to be said. Then she realized, in that moment, that it was the perfect time to tell Mitch about Charlie. It was time for her to be honest, not just about her feelings but about her old family friend.

"Mitch, there's something really important that I want to talk to you about," she said while holding Mitch's hand, her voice filled with emotion. "You know, I'm glad you didn't get that corporate job. I prefer the simpler life we lead now. Before, we lived in a big house and the money was good, but you worked so hard and there was no time for us. And, as well-taken care of as we were, I don't think that corporate job left you feeling fulfilled."

Sandy continued. "I long for the days when we were first married, when we were happy even though we didn't have a lot. Life was simpler, you were a gifted teacher, you came home early every day and we had long dinners with inspiring conversations full of laughter. We shared our hopes and dreams. We had

time for wonderful holidays and weekends together."
By this time, Sandy could barely hold back the tears!

The unexpected response from Sandy left Mitch
speechless.

But Sandy was not done yet. "There's something else
I've wanted to tell you. You know the journal you've
been getting these great recipes from? It belongs to
my friend Charlie, who's been a part of my family
for a very long time, since the days of Great Grandpa
Henry." As soon as Mitch heard "Grandpa Henry",
he quickly hid his ring-less hand under the table.
Sandy went on to tell Mitch the family legend of
Charlie and Grandpa Henry's first encounter.

"That's the story of how Happy Houses came to be.
It was all thanks to Charlie's and Grandpa Henry's
compassionate hearts. Since then, although our
family business was thriving, what has remained
most important to us wasn't the money that it
brought, but the sense of satisfaction we got from
helping others, the pride we took in our work and
all the lives that we touched. Charlie's caring heart
inspired our family so much, I'm so grateful he's here
with us. When you get to know him, you'll get to see
how great Charlie is."

Just then, Mitch heard a loud snap from behind the
stove, one of the traps had gone off.

"What was that?" Sandy asked.

Mitch quickly changed the subject and pleaded, "This is all too much for me; let's go to bed."

"Wait, not yet. I want you to meet Charlie," Sandy insisted. "Charlie! Come out, Mitch wants to meet you" Sandy called. They waited but there was no sign of Charlie. Mitch was horrified as his mind raced a million miles an hour; he had lost the ring and killed the mouse, the family's two most valued treasures. He could feel the sweat forming on his forehead as his heart pounded loudly.

"It's alright; let's do this another night Sandy," Mitch urged as he began to feel sick in the pit of his stomach.

"Charlie, there's someone here that I want you to meet," Sandy called out again. Still, there was no sign of Charlie. "I don't get it, I hope he's okay," Sandy sighed.

Mitch fretted and insisted again. "Sandy, let's go to bed."

Worried about Mitch's frazzled behavior, Sandy asked, "Are you okay? What's wrong?"

Just then, poking out from behind the stove,

a small head with big ears slowly appeared. Mitch's face turned pale and his eyes grew wide as if he had seen a ghost. Sandy knelt down on the floor and extended her hand as Charlie ran to her.

"Charlie, I'd like you to meet my husband, Mitch," Sandy said as she held Charlie up. Charlie looked at Mitch and gracefully took a bow while Mitch stared, still in disbelief.

"Charlie is a very clever mouse; he's the one who left the journal for you to find in hopes that you might accept him as your friend. You know, he can help us both," Sandy told Mitch as Charlie's eyes sparkled with eagerness.

This all seemed a bit too far fetched to Mitch. His anger dissolved but he still wasn't ready to believe the crazy story. He thought to himself, "First of all, how could a mouse read and write? Mice don't read and write! And then she says he planted a garden during the Great Depression? If that story were true, then he's got to be 88 years old at least! And he's supposed to help us?! I don't need help, especially not from a mouse. How insulting."

Mitch abruptly pushed his chair back and got up from the table. "Sandy, this is all too much for me to take in. I'm going to bed early tonight," he said as he rushed off to bed, weary, and his head spinning with the strange events of the day.

CHAPTER ELEVEN
CHARLIE'S AMBITIOUS IDEA

*"For myself I am an optimist – it does not seem to
be much use being anything else."*
–Sir Winston Churchill

As Mitch retreated to the bedroom, Charlie and
Sandy looked knowingly at each other in silence.
They knew this reaction was normal. It would be a
challenge for Mitch to accept Charlie's existence,
but eventually he would come around to it. Charlie
was optimistic as he began brainstorming ways for
Sandy and Mitch to reconnect.

Sandy apologized to Charlie for Mitch's behavior.
Then she bid Charlie good night and went off to
bed. The little mouse stood still for a second and
then scampered across the counter, back to his home
in the wall. Once home, he thought about how he
would go about returning the ring to Mitch without
letting Sandy find out. He needed a place where only
Mitch would see it.

BAM! Lost in thought, Charlie had not even
noticed the pair of leather shoes Mitch had been
wearing that morning. He crashed into them and lay
on the ground, seeing a few stars around his head.

But then, he had a great idea. "Aha! His shoes! The perfect place!" Charlie thought.

He rushed back home, retrieved the ring and wrote a short note to go along with it. He eagerly returned to the shoe and placed the ring inside, leaving his note:

Dear Mitch,
All is Possible.
- Charlie

Satisfied with his idea, Charlie returned to his hole and lay down to sleep, excited to see Mitch after he would find the ring in the morning.

But Mitch woke up the next day in a foul mood. He hadn't been able to sleep from thinking of the fact that he had lost his wedding ring. He felt horrible about it. Sandy was at work and he was alone in the house as usual. After wandering the house aimlessly for a few minutes, he decided to go out for breakfast and take a break from his daily routine. Maybe that would get his mind off his current situation, at least for a little bit.

After changing out of his pajamas, he put on his shoes and prepared to go out. "Ouch! What's that?" Mitch yelled. Something in his shoe was digging into his heel every time he stepped down. He sat back down and took his shoes off to investigate. Turning his shoe upside down, Mitch saw a small silver thing drop onto the floor with a tiny clink. It was his wedding ring! Mitch was jubilant! But how had the ring gotten here? He remembered accidently dropping it into the drain yesterday. Once again, Mitch was puzzled; he was finding himself in this state quite often these days.

Further examining the shoe, Mitch found that there was also a note in it. And it was signed by Charlie. But Mitch was not interested in playing such games this early in the morning. "Whatever. I'm hungry," Mitch said. He placed the note on the counter mindlessly, got into his car and drove to his favorite breakfast café, eager to get away from the cottage. On the way, he tried to make sense of all the recent events, thinking, "I wish my life were normal again."

At the café, Mitch sat down to a heaping plate of sausages, scrambled eggs and hash browns. To top it all off, he devoured a stack of pancakes smothered in syrup. While Mitch was at breakfast, Charlie spent some time turning some Thinking Cheese over in his paws; the cheese was part of the stash that he stowed away for dire situations. He felt like this was exactly one of those situations.

He smelled the cheese, letting the aroma fill his eager nose, letting his whiskers twitch out of sheer delight. Just the smell warmed his heart and reminded him of everything good in the world. If a smell this good was possible, then ALL things must be possible! All of a sudden, he had a perfect plan for how to bring Sandy and Mitch close again while helping them both! Finally, he tilted his head back and triumphantly dropped the bit of cheese right in.

With his stomach full, Mitch returned home. He had overeaten and laid down on the sofa to watch TV. But although he was content that his belly was full, Mitch felt a sense of emptiness and despair as he thought about his future. It looked gloomy from where he was sitting. His dreams of living a life of grandeur and abundance seemed so out of reach.

Poking out of his hole, Charlie could see Mitch sinking deeper into depression. Charlie was compelled with a sense of urgency to put his plan into action. He scurried around the house, searching for a sheet of paper—no luck. Determined, he found a brown paper bag, took it apart so that it formed a large sheet and got to work.

At that moment, Mitch got up from the couch and went into the kitchen to make a cup of coffee, hoping that it might lift his spirits. As he looked blankly out of the kitchen window, he spotted Charlie in the backyard scurrying about and seemingly examining every inch of it. The little mouse seemed to be intently making notes on a sheet of paper. Completely amazed to see the mouse writing with a tiny pencil, Mitch rubbed his eyes to check if he was dreaming. But he was wide awake.

"What is this mouse doing?" Mitch grumbled, half intrigued and half resentful of his presence.

After leaving the garden, Charlie spent hours scribbling endless notes and drawing detailed pictures. Finally his masterpiece was complete.

The next morning, Sandy slipped on her jacket and walked out the door heading to work. Feeling for the keys in her jacket pocket, she found a surprise. Charlie had left a note and a large piece of brown paper rolled up with a piece of twine tied in a bow. The note, in Charlie's distinctive handwriting, read:

Dear Sandy,
There's a light at the end of the garden! We will raise the spirits of Mitch and bring a hope that will spread. We're going to plant a garden! I'm going to call it the Garden of Life.
- Charlie

Sandy was a little confused. "Why does Charlie want to plant a garden? How is this going to help the situation with Mitch? Well, I don't know what Charlie has in mind, but I bet he's got a clever idea in the making." Sandy unrolled the brown paper to find a detailed diagram of the backyard converted into a vegetable and herb garden.

"Wow! Charlie must have spent days making this, there's so much detail," she thought as she imagined her backyard's wildly growing weeds replaced by delicious and colorful vegetables. For a moment, Sandy stopped to reminisce about her fond childhood memories in the family garden.

On another piece of brown paper, Sandy found detailed instructions for starting the Garden of Life and a shopping list of the materials needed.

The Garden of Life

As flowers will open the heart, our hands in the soil will connect us to the earth. Our minds and hearts will unite as one, opening up possibilities that extend far beyond the horizon to illuminate our unique role in the world.

There will be 7 sections of vegetables and herbs in the garden. Here's what you need to create the Garden of Life.

Shopping List for Gardening 101

56 different kinds of vegetables
22 different kinds of herbs
20 different kinds of fruit trees
3 different flowers
And a collection of hand tools

Everything you need for the Garden of Life!

The notes continued, detailing all the plants that would be planted and where they would go. "There are seven sections, this is huge! I think Charlie is getting too ambitious here. It would take Mitch and me more than two weekends just to do one section. That is, if I could manage to get Mitch to help. I guess I can pick up some materials on my way home from work and get started on the first section," Sandy thought as she left the house.

That afternoon, Mitch was moping around the house as usual. He entered the kitchen, getting ready to prepare a fourth dinner from the journal. Then he noticed another worn leather-bound book sitting on the countertop, in the same place where he had left Charlie's note. Mitch stood over it and thought, "What a curious book, I wonder if this is Sandy's?" He picked it up and read its faded title, *All is Possible*. Mitch carefully leafed through the delicate pages and discovered a tiny note:

This is my favorite book, I hope you like it.

Completely bewildered, Mitch's thoughts darted back and forth several times between the book and the note. Sandy knew he didn't read much, so he couldn't understand why she would give him the book. "What is Sandy doing? She's trying to make me believe that a mouse can read and write? Ugh! This is too much for me! I think I'm going to have that fruit salad Sandy made last night," Mitch exclaimed.

He decided to ignore the book, strolled languidly into the kitchen and opened the refrigerator door. To his disappointment, all that was left was an empty container, no fruit in sight. "Sandy must have eaten it," he reasoned. Still, there was a lingering doubt in the back of his mind about whether the mouse had eaten it.

"But why would a mouse get in a refrigerator and climb up three shelves to that particular container when there were lower shelves with plenty of delicious food in them? And if the mouse did go for that particular container of food then he must have had a reason..."

Mitch spent several minutes in front of the open refrigerator door rationalizing his missing fruit before he suddenly yelled, "I've had enough of this!" And he meant all of it—always finding his favorite desserts gone, stories of mice who could read and write, the strange notes that he had been finding. There

were no such things as mice that could read or write!
He picked up the phone and dialed Sandy at work.

"Did you eat that fruit salad in the refrigerator?"
Mitch asked, breathless and very disturbed.

"Well, hello to you too. And, no. You said you
wanted it," Sandy replied.

"It's gone," Mitch fumed.

"Charlie must have eaten it," she dismissed.

This was more than he could handle. He hung up
the phone abruptly, walked back into the living
room and fell into the couch. His face buried in the
sofa, Mitch tried to fight back tears of frustration at
all the events of recent weeks. How could all of this
be happening to him? What had become of his life?

Sandy was late coming home that night. She'd made
a stop at the local nursery and picked up a few
things. On the way home, she called Mitch to let
him know that she was running late because she had
bought a bunch of things for the house and asked
him if he would help unload the car when she got
home.

Mitch, slowly recovering from his very emotionally
draining afternoon, looked forward to seeing what
Sandy had gotten for the house. As Mitch went to

the car to help Sandy unload, he was disappointed to see gardening tools and bags of soil.

"What's all this for?" he asked Sandy.

"Oh, I thought we could plant a garden," she responded with excitement.

"A garden? Where did you get that idea from?" Mitch asked.

Knowing that Mitch would resent the real source, Sandy replied, "I grew up with gardens in my home and I miss it, so I thought we could plant one together in the backyard. It'll be fun."

CHAPTER TWELVE
THE GARDEN OF LIFE

"We cannot always build the future for our youth, but we can build our youth for the future." – Franklin D. Roosevelt

The next day, Sandy woke up bright and early and went outside with an old t-shirt and jeans, ready to begin weeding the garden. She had tried to get Mitch to join her, but he quickly abandoned the work and retreated to the porch. After Sandy had been weeding for a quite a while, an unexpected little voice caused her to turn halfway around. A young girl stood looking over the fence. She and her grandmother had been watching from their porch next door and she had come over to ask Sandy what she was doing.

"I'm making a garden," Sandy said.

"Really? With flowers and vegetables an' stuff?" asked the little girl, excitedly.

"Yes! But mostly just good, wholesome, delicious vegetables. Say, you wouldn't want to help me would you?" Sandy asked.

"CAN I??" The little girl's eyes lit up.

Sandy replied, "Of course you can. Run and ask your mom if it's okay."

The little girl dropped her head down and muttered, "I can't."

"Can't what, sweetie?" asked Sandy, concerned.

"Can't ask my mom. She...she died. I live with my grandma now." Sandy was quiet for a moment as she looked at the top of the little girl's head. Smiling warmly, she bent down and said, "Well, then go ask your grandmother if you can help me. I really need someone who's closer to the ground than I am to get these seeds planted properly."

She ran over to her grandmother, then came running back with a huge smile on her face. "Grandma says it's okay for me to help you in your garden."

"That's great! My name's Sandy, what's your name?"

"I'm Sylvia," the little girl said, smiling shyly.

All that afternoon, Sylvia and Sandy toiled happily in the garden plot. Mitch gave up shortly after the digging portion and begrudgingly watched from the porch. "All that hard work. Dusty, dirty, and muddy. What is enjoyable about that?" Mitch thought. Just one hour of back-breaking labor would have been enough for Mitch. He was even more convinced that he'd been right. All this work when you could just simply go out and BUY the vegetables! He just didn't get it. Finally, he couldn't take it anymore and retreated back into the house.

Sylvia bent down to pull up a weed and yanked off the top. Sandy stopped what she was doing to sit down next to her. "Sylvia, sweetie, when you pull up a weed, you have to pull up the entire weed, right down to the root. When you just take off the top, you leave that root to keep growing back. You see, weeds are like problems; clear off the surface, and it may LOOK like they're handled, but if you don't get to the root, they'll come again when you least expect it. And they'll come up twice as strong because they've had that much more time to grow."

Sylvia looked at the leaves in her hand and frowned. She went to the weed she'd tried to pull and dug down into the soil. When she got hold of the root, she pulled and pulled. When it came out, it knocked her on her back with the force of her tugging.

Giggling, she held it up for Sandy to see. "I GOT it!!" she declared excitedly. Sandy giggled right along with her. Mitch watched, with his comfortable disdain, but the scene was silly enough to bring a smile even to his mouth.

"Where should I put the weeds after I pull them up?" Sylvia asked. She proudly carried a pile of dirty weeds, properly yanked up, roots and all.

"I've got a compost pile started behind the house; you could set them there."

"What's a compost pile?"

Sandy grinned. "It's a pile of rotten vegetables, wilted flowers, moldy bread and any other kind of vegetarian stuff that would go in the garbage. You put it in a pile, add some water and a few worms and it starts to decompose."

"That sounds gross, Sandy."

"It's not gross! Well, okay, it's a little gross, but it's nutritious for the vegetables. It helps make the soil more fertile. Think of it as the cycle of life: the plants grow up, they die and then they go back into the earth where they came from and add nutrients and food to the soil so new plants can thrive."

Sylvia nodded. "Cool, I'll go put the weeds on the compost pile!"

As Sandy picked up her shovel, she noticed a note tucked underneath it:

You brighten lives
by opening hearts and minds
to endless possibilities.

Looking up from the note, Sandy noticed Charlie sitting up in the black walnut tree, enjoying a leafy green as he held a pencil in his other paw.

Sandy walked over to where Charlie was and asked him if he wanted to meet Sylvia. "She's such a sweet little angel."

Charlie nodded excitedly. Just then, Sylvia walked over and asked inquisitively, "What are you doing now?"

"Sylvia, do you think you can keep a secret?"

Sylvia's eyes went wide. "Boy, can I keep secrets! I keep all kinds of secrets! Like my Grandma has a secret about Mr. Higgins..."

"Oh, good, good, well, don't tell me! I'll introduce you to my friend, but you have to keep him secret."
"I promise!" Sylvia pronounced earnestly.

Sandy called Charlie over to meet Sylvia. "Charlie, this is my gardening angel, Sylvia. Sylvia, I'd like you to meet Charlie."

Charlie bowed another one of his graceful bows from his place on the tree as his eyes met Sylvia's.

Excited, Sylvia asked, "Can I hold him? He's so adorable in his jacket!"

"He would love for you to hold him. Be careful, he's small."

Sandy reached her hand up to Charlie and he quickly hopped right on. She gently brought him down and placed him in Sylvia's hands.

"Hello, Charlie," Sylvia said. "You're the cutest mouse I've EVER seen! And I've never seen a jacket as nice as yours." Sylvia extended an index finger to gently stroke Charlie's pretty jacket, but suddenly froze mid-air and gave out a little, tiny shriek.

"Sylvia, what's wrong?" Sandy asked. "There's a bee!" Sylvia whispered. A bee had come to hover right around Charlie and she froze, afraid of startling the bee and accidentally getting stung.

"Oh, Sylvia, you must be good luck!" Sandy gently exclaimed. "I am?" Sylvia replied. "Why, yes! Our garden needs bees, and you found one. Bees are very special. Plants and bees have a unique relationship. Without each other, neither one would ever exist. And then what would we eat?"

Just then, the bee flew away in search of something appetizing. Sylvia dropped her tired arm that had held up her frozen hand. Wiping her brow with a dramatic, "Whew!" and handing Charlie back to Sandy, Sylvia asked, "What do you mean bees and plants wouldn't exist?"

Sandy gently lifted Charlie back up to the tree and kneeled down in front of a bright yellow dandelion, motioning to Sylvia to do the same. "Flowers make pollen. Pollen is like a gourmet dinner for bees. It has all the vitamins, minerals, fats and proteins that bees need to be healthy—all in one place. When the bee comes to eat, tiny bits of pollen stick to the bees so when they go to their next meal, some of the pollen on their body falls off. This happens over and over again as the bees fly around to different plants and flowers, leaving pollen everywhere they go."

"They're messy ea ers!" Sylvia exclaimed, giggling. "Yes, bu it's a good mess," Sandy continued, "because then the plants and flowers become fertilized by the pollen from other plants and flow- ers."

"What does fertilized mean?"

"Well, it means the plants and flowers can now make their own fruits and seeds."

"You mean, without pollen an apple tree couldn't make any apples?"

"Yes, and without the apple tree's flowers, there

would be no food for the bees."

"Then there would be no bees to bring the pollen!"

"That's right! See why bees are good luck, and why they're our very special friends?"

"I get it now. I hope that bee we saw brings friends!"

"Why don't we get started growing stuff for them, and maybe their whole family will come!"

Sylvia jumped up and squealed, "Okay!" excited to see another bee. She ran back to where they had been working and pulled weeds with a newfound excitement.

Several hours passed before Mitch peeked outside to find that not only was Sandy still working in the garden, but she had attracted even more company. Two young boys had joined Sylvia and it looked like a lively conversation was going on between them. Mitch cracked the window to hear.

"So, how can I help with gardening?" asked one of the boys. Mitch looked at the kids. The closer one appeared to be about 12 years old and full of curiosity under his head of curls. But from the looks he kept shooting young Sylvia, he was a bit smitten. Mitch faintly recognized him as the school headache from his teaching days. The other boy was a little younger and somewhat on the shy side.

"Well, making a garden takes a lot of work and you have to learn how to pull out weeds the right way." Sylvia looked at the two boys. "Want me to show you?" The two kids looked at each other, shrugged their shoulders and bent down to see what Sylvia was doing.

On his afternoon walk, Mr. Smith, a distinguished gentleman with white hair, wire rim glasses, a moustache and a passion for gardening stopped outside the fence to see if he could offer some advice or assistance. Soon, he too, was weeding away as he warmly shared his wisdom with the youngsters. For the rest of the afternoon, the group continued to work in the garden, telling jokes and laughing, playing games and having a great time. When the sun finally went down, the eager helpers were sad to leave and each one promised to return the next morning. As Sandy stood in her garden waving goodbye to her new friends a sense of contentment filled her spirit and her soul.

The next day everyone was back bright and early. Mr. Smith was weeding with the boys. Sylvia, Sandy and Charlie were starting on the next steps to making the garden plant-ready. This endearing scene secretly enraptured Mitch from his warm seat by the window. He had even cracked open the window to hear what they were laughing and talking about.

The boys were asking Mr. Smith about what the right way to pull weeds was. Mitch heard Mr. Smith say, "Boys, you have to dig down deep to loosen the soil around the roots. You have to focus to pull the whole weed up, including the roots" animating the process with his voice and hand gestures. He continued, "That way you take care of the whole thing and the weed can't come back. It's like the problems you face in your own life. If you focus on them one at a time and fix them at the root, you won't have to worry about it coming up again." As Mitch listened, he caught Sylvia and Sandy eavesdropping on Mr. Smith and the boys' conversation. Suddenly, the girls exchanged glances and began giggling uncontrollably.

Before long, Sandy had them all making furrows and running water down the rows. Everyone was getting really dirty but seemed to be having a great time. Mitch didn't get it. He knew that no weekend getaway would bring an expression to Sandy's face like the one she wore now. As romantic and wonderful as it would have been, it wouldn't have put the color in her cheeks and the laughter in her voice these past hours had done.

Words of Wisdom
Charlie's Favorite Quotes

"Work is love made visible." – Kahlil Gibran

"There is no such thing as a problem without a gift for you in its hands. You seek problems because you need their gifts." – Richard Bach

"Of a certainty the man who can see all creatures in himself, knows no sorrow." – Eesha Upanishad

"A child's life is like a piece of paper on which every passerby leaves a mark." – Ancient Chinese Proverb

"You can do it if you think you can." – Napoleon Hill

"We are free to go where we wish and be what we are." – Richard Bach

"If you don't live the life you believe - you will believe the life you live." – Author Unknown

"The way you see life will largely determine what you will get out of it." – Zig Ziglar

"Most people are just as happy as they make their minds up to be." – Abraham Lincoln

"As a man thinketh in his heart, so is he." – Proverbs 23:7

CHAPTER THIRTEEN
CHARLIE'S NEW FRIENDS

*"Beautiful young people are accidents of nature,
but beautiful old people are works of art."*
– Eleanor Roosevelt

The laughter and fun was suddenly disturbed by a shrieking, "Sandy, Sandy come look at this!" Hearing Sylvia's distress, Sandy, Mr. Smith and the boys all went running to the compost pile.

"What's wrong Sylvia, are you okay?" Sylvia pointed to something moving in the compost pile, "What's that? It looks awfully frightening!"

Everyone looked over and saw a millipede crawling in the compost pile.

"Wow. Cool!" shouted the older boy. "It's like an alien!"

"It's gross," Sylvia stated humorlessly.

"Oh, Sylvia, it's not gross, it's just a bug," Sandy comforted her. "He won't hurt you."

"Millipedes are good for the garden. They help break up dead and dying plants and they eat nasty bugs that want to eat the seedlings. They help in recycling and decomposing bacteria and fungi," Mr. Smith added.

"But it's scary," Sylvia said.

"He's probably more afraid of you than you could ever be of him, Sylvia. Imagine how scary you must look to him. You're a giant!" Everyone began laughing and fondly teasing Sylvia.

Sylvia blushed, bashfully biting her lip and dropping her chin to her chest. She was afraid of bugs and wasn't used to being teased and laughed at. She tucked her hands into her pockets, suddenly embarrassed, when she discovered an unfamiliar slip of folded paper inside one of her pockets. She pulled it out and discovered a handwritten note, which read:

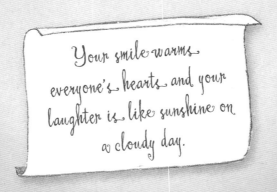

Your smile warms everyone's hearts and your laughter is like sunshine on a cloudy day.

After reading it, she began to giggle as she wondered who could've possibly put it in there. She smiled big enough for everyone to see as thanks for her secret note. This made everyone around smile with her and soon the laughter started up again.

In the midst of the laughing, Mr. Smith saw a friend walking by and waved to the equally energetic elderly man, Mr. Higgins. "Come join us, Higgins," Mr. Smith shouted.

"Gardening, huh Smith? What are you teaching these youngsters? I'll help out just to make sure you're teaching them the right stuff," Mr. Higgins joked with a bright smile.

Just then, Sandy walked over with the map of the Garden of Life in hand to welcome Mr. Higgins. "It's a pleasure to see you here, Mr. Higgins. I'm so pleased that you're joining us in the garden," Sandy said with a smile.

"The pleasure is mine. You know I've got to keep an eye on my old friend Smith, here."

Sandy began to unroll the map in her hand. "So this is the plan for the garden." Mr. Higgins and Mr. Smith's eyes lit up as they carefully studied the map in awe.

"This is genius! See how the vegetables are in beds

and not in rows? Big men like us could ruin the soil structure if we had to walk in between rows, so using beds is brilliant. And look at these combinations—basil and tomato, raspberries and garlic, sweet peppers and squash. Did you know they all grow in perfect harmony, nourishing each other's soil and repelling each other's pests? Reminds me of a good ol' fashioned friendship! The Garden of Life! Whoever thought of it gave it a fitting name," Mr. Smith complimented.

"Who's the mastermind behind this? Did you do this Sandy? It's inspired. Who would have thought to plant these combinations of vegetables that are so compatible and complementary to each other?" Higgins exclaimed.

"Oh, Charlie made it..." Sandy caught herself midsentence.

"Who's Charlie?" they both asked inquisitively.

"Uh oh, now I have some explaining to do" Sandy thought. "Charlie's a very old friend of mine," she said.

"Oh, I would love to meet him," Smith interrupted.

"Yeah, me too. This guy must be something special," Higgins added.

"Yes, he's very special. Maybe almost unbelievable. You have to have a very open mind to appreciate him."

The two men nodded eagerly. "Now you really have me intrigued," Mr. Smith said. "I'd really like to meet the little guy."

"He's a very little guy and he's kind of my little secret, but I think you guys would understand. Just wait here," Sandy said and went to the walnut tree.

Meanwhile, Sylvia had been trying to get her grandmother to come over to help. "Come on grandma, I want to show you the garden. Oh look, there's Mr. Higgins and Mr. Smith. Let's go say hi to them," Sylvia said as she pulled her grandmother's hands and walked her over.

"Oh, Sylvia, you've come at just the perfect time. Let's share our little secret with Mr. Higgins, Mr. Smith and your grandma," Sandy whispered into Sylvia's ear.

Excitedly clapping her hands and jumping up and down, Sylvia could barely contain herself.

Sandy and Sylvia beckoned Mr. Smith and Mr. Higgins over to meet Sylvia's grandmother and Charlie. Charlie was excitedly waiting, dressed in his jacket and with a pencil in his paw. Sylvia lifted him from

his place on the tree and held him before the two
gentlemen and her grandmother.

"I'd like you all to meet Charlie. Charlie, please meet
my grandmother, Mr. Smith and Mr. Higgins."
Charlie took a little bow with a big smile.

Slowly, Mr. Higgins allowed a grin to creep over his face. "You're telling me this little guy is the architect behind this amazing garden?"

Sandy proudly nodded. "He's a very special mouse."

"Indeed, he is," Mr. Smith nearly shouted.

"Good to meet you, little fella!" Mr. Higgins laughed.

Charlie swelled with delight, excited to make new friends.

"You won't believe what this little guy cooked up. As a gourmet food lover, you would be pleased with this clever little guy's map of the garden," Mr. Higgins commented to Sylvia's grandmother.

"Oh, what a pleasure it is to meet you Charlie," Sylvia's grandmother said.

"You're just full of surprises, Sandy," Mr. Smith said.

"It's certainly been a very special day," Mr. Higgins added.

Words of Wisdom
Charlie's Favorite Quotes

"Miracles happen to those who believe in them."
– Bernard Berenson

"Life is partly what we make it, and partly what it is made by the friends we choose."
– Tennessee Williams

"A healthy social life is found only, when in the mirror of each soul the whole community finds its reflection, and when in the whole community the virtue of each one is living." – Rudolph Steiner

"What should young people do with their lives today? Many things, obviously. But the most daring thing is to create stable communities in which the terrible disease of loneliness can be cured." – Kurt Vonnegut, Jr.

"The strongest bond of human sympathy outside the family relation should be one uniting working people of all nations and tongues and kindreds." – Abraham Lincoln

"Truly great friends are hard to find, difficult to leave, and impossible to forget." – Author Unknown

"If you will practice being fictional for a while, you will understand that fictional characters are sometimes more real than people with bodies and heartbeats." – Richard Bach

CHAPTER FOURTEEN
MITCH VENTURES OUT

"One thing life has taught me: if you are interested, you never have to look for new interests. They come to you. When you are genuinely interested in one thing, it will always lead to something else." –Eleanor Roosevelt.

Like the day before, Mitch could hear the busy sounds and voices out in the garden when he woke up. He sighed. The last day of the weekend and it looked like yard work was still the order of the day. He got up, showered, dressed and stood beside the window looking out over the garden. The sun shone brightly overhead.

Mitch was shocked to see a small crowd bustling back and forth among the weeds and dirt. In the early morning, the garden had filled with many pairs of helping hands. Sandy stood in one corner studying Charlie's plans for the garden. Mr. Smith and Mr. Higgins were involved in a colorful conversation with the children, planning what they would do in the garden that day.

"Right over here, kids. We'll plant the orange and purple carrots next to the cabbage and chervil," Mr. Higgins instructed.

"Wow! Purple carrots?! Those aren't real...! Are they? And what's chervil?" asked Sylvia.

"Purple carrots have been around as long as Egyptian times, about 2,000 years. Dark vegetables like purple carrots are packed with antioxidants that protect our hearts and protect us from cancer. In southern Europe, black, red, yellow and white carrots were also grown in the 14th century. Orange carrots came from Holland and they're rich in beta-carotene that becomes vitamin A in our body and helps us see better in the dark. If you slice a carrot, you'll see that it even looks like the human eye," Mr. Smith explained.

"Cool! I can't wait to taste it!" the children shouted.

"And chervil is a neat little herb related to parsley. It helps protect the cabbage from bugs and also tastes great as seasoning," continued Mr. Smith. "Tell us more, tell us more," the children begged, hungry for more facts about vegetables. "Well," he said, "who wants to learn how to grow cotton candy in the garden?"

"You can't GROW cotton candy," the children exclaimed, almost in unison. "They make that in a big machine, like at the fair," proclaimed the older boy, quite proudly. "That's true, son, but how about the ORIGINAL cotton candy?" quizzed Mr. Higgins, with a wink directed at Mr. Smith. The older boy looked around at the other kids, but nobody knew the answer. Mr. Smith continued. "Cotton candy is actually a super-sweet variety of corn, sweeter than you've ever tasted! And you can grow it right in your own backyard."

"Just wait," Mr. Higgins added. "Once you've tried it, you'll know what cotton candy really tastes like!" The kids bubbled over with excitement at this new fun fact while Mr. Smith and Mr. Higgins smiled gleefully at one another. Planting seeds of knowledge in young minds was just as fun as planting seeds in a garden!

From his window, Mitch had been watching and listening in to the conversations. It was good that the children were learning, but he still didn't understand this gardening thing. Everyone was outside digging and working hard. He hated this kind of manual labor. But everyone outside seemed to be enjoying themselves. "Why are they having such a great time?" Mitch thought.

Below, in the garden, Sandy was trying to break the hard soil and looked up to see Mitch staring from the window. Sandy sighed sadly. Charlie, who had seen Sandy's longing gaze at the bedroom window, tugged at her pant leg, pointed to the hard ground and then pointed to Mitch.

Sandy snapped her fingers and said, "Good idea, Charlie." She headed toward the house to tell him they needed his help.

"Honey, I would love it if you could help us outside. You're a big, strong...caveman. I'll bet you could break the harder soil a lot faster than I can. It would really help me, Mitch. Would you?" Sandy had to go on for a couple of minutes before Mitch would agree to change into his jeans and work boots and venture out into the garden.

As Mitch and Sandy walked back to the garden, Sylvia scampered up to Sandy, stopping her in her tracks to ask, "Where's he going with that giant fork?" Sandy giggled in reply, "That's a garden fork. He's going to break up the hard soil. When the soil's too hard we can't plant any seeds." Sylvia asked,

"Can't we just wet the soil to make it soft?" Surprised, Sandy replied, "Well aren't you smart! Yes, we could, but the vegetables I'm planting there are root vegetables that grow underground. Those need lots of room to stretch out and grow." Sylvia exclaimed, "Just like me! Grandma says I need a bigger bed now because I'm growing and I like to stretch out when I sleep." Laughing, Sandy said, "That's absolutely right," as she grabbed Sylvia's hand and walked with her back to the garden.

The children began busily digging furrows under the guidance of Mr. Smith, closely following the metrics outlined in Charlie's map. Sandy and Mitch diligently broke the soil. Mr. Higgins noticed Mitch's presence in the garden and strolled over to welcome him.

"Why, hello Mitch! It's good to see you out here. We really needed a strong hand. You really know how to get that ground loosened up," Higgins said as he warmly greeted Mitch. "I've been wondering what took you so long to come join us."

"Gardening isn't really my thing, I guess. And I haven't been feeling motivated to do much of anything since I got laid off," Mitch replied.

"Oh, that. I got laid off lots of times—got fired once or twice, too!" he laughed. "It's all part of living. I would have been bored stiff working the same job all my life. You got to have a hobby, at least. If you've got a good, constructive hobby, you'll go places. None of this sitting in front of the TV, letting your brain turn to compost. You might be surprised at how much you'll like gardening. When I was your age, I thought gardening was only for old people. Then I started doing it."

"Hmm...maybe, I'll give it some time," Mitch responded, glad that Mr. Higgins could relate to his situation.

Someone tapped Mr. Higgins on the shoulder as he was mid-conversation with Mitch. When he turned, Sandy was holding a tall glass of iced lemonade. Sylvia had been beckoned home by her grandmother, Ms. Contadino, who wanted to make a treat for the crew. They brought it over together in a big canister in Sylvia's little wagon along with a stack of paper cups. It was a good time for everyone to take a break and enjoy the sweet lemonade.

"I've got this great big lemon tree in my backyard. Grows more lemons than I could ever use," Sylvia's grandmother exclaimed as she sat to the side and watched everybody savor the moment as they cooled off with the lemonade.

Everyone took turns acknowledging Sylvia's grandmother's kindness and perfect lemonade. Sylvia beamed with pride. Mr. Higgins boldly walked over to Sylvia's grandmother, who was still sitting in the shade.

"I swear, nobody makes lemonade like you do. It's got just the right balance of tartness and sweetness. But there's something I can't quite put my finger on...," he said.

"I'll let you in on a little secret from the old country. I add a touch of mint to my famous lemonade, a family tradition," she whispered. "But that's our little secret," she said with a smile and a wink.

They continued their lively conversation with frequent spurts of laughter from both sides. As Higgins was nearing the bottom of his lemonade, he asked her if she wanted to help with gardening.

He smoothly pulled the question off as Smith happened to overhear him and yelled, "Yea, we could use another hand and we would love your help." The next thing she knew, Sylvia's grandmother had a hose in her hand with Sylvia on one side and Mr. Higgins on the other. Not only was she enjoying the work, but she was taking the lead with her gardening wisdom.

"You plant basil and tomatoes together, because they both put nutrients back into the soil that the other plant needs. Isn't that useful? And then, when they're ripe, basil and tomatoes taste fantastic together! It's like they were designed that way. When these seedlings mature, I'll make my special tomato and basil sandwich with olive oil and mozzarella, a heavenly combination," she shared.

Charlie's taste buds tickled as he sipped from his helping of lemonade. The mouse nearly fell out of his hiding place in the tree while he scribbled a note of appreciation:

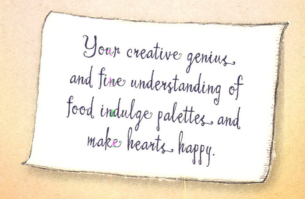

Your creative genius and fine understanding of food indulge palettes and make hearts happy.

Charlie slipped the note into Sylvia's grandmother's apron. She later discovered it to much surprise and delight. A warm smile spread from her face to the rest of her body as she wondered who could have written the note.

As Mr. Higgins returned to where he had set down his lemonade, he too discovered a little note next to his glass:

> Your kind words and compassionate understanding give encouragement and create possibilities where there were none.

A curious smile came over his face as he wondered where the uplifting and mysterious note could have come from.

Words of Wisdom
Charlie's Favorite Quotes

"Every gift from a friend is a wish for your happiness." – Richard Bach

"When your heart is in your dreams, no request is too extreme." – Jiminy Cricket

"You can't always get what you want, but if you try sometimes, you might find, you get what you need." – The Rolling Stones

"What old people say you cannot do, you try and find that you can. Old deeds for old people, and new deeds for new." – Henry David Thoreau

"Other things may change us, but we start and end with family." – Anthony Brandt

"Keep your heart open to dreams. For as long as there's a dream, there is hope, and as long as there is hope, there is joy in living." – Author Unknown

"To look backward for a while is to refresh the eye, to restore it, and to render it the more fit for its prime function of looking forward." – Margaret Fairless Barber

"We will only understand the miracle of life fully when we allow the unexpected to happen." – Paulo Coelho

CHAPTER FIFTEEN
ALL IS POSSIBLE!

*"You're always free to change your mind and choose
a different future, or a different past."*
–Richard Bach

In another part of the garden, Mr. Smith sat down next to Mitch as he was finishing his lemonade.

"You know, I've been watching you. I'm guessing you weren't all that keen on working in the garden at first, am I right?"

Mitch nodded, slowly.

"You probably thought it was for old geezers like us." Mitch let out a laugh.

"Thought so. I've talked with Sandy a bit. Mind you, she wasn't really telling any tales out of school. But I'm a keen old buster and I know a thing or two. She said you'd started out as a teacher. Well, I can see that. You're kind of a natural at it. You had those kids asking questions and you answering them pretty much all day. They like being around you and, whether you realize it or not, young man, *you* like being around *them*. Now, I know you've lost your big fancy job and that's eating away at you some. And I know what that's like. I worked for a company. Worked my heart out. Worked more hours than I probably should have, considering the outcome. Without one word of warning, one day the boss came in, handed me my envelope with the pink slip inside and helped me pack up the desk that I'd called my home away from home for almost 10 years. Downsizing wasn't the word they used for it in those days, but a trip out the door is still a trip out the door. They gave me two week's pay, a lousy sorry and a handshake. The next thing I knew I was walking my box and myself to the car. I was mad as the dickens. Scared too. Two week's pay isn't much when you've got a house to pay for and mouths to feed. And I didn't have one idea what I was going to do from there." Mr. Smith paused, pensively.

"But I was lucky, Mitch," he continued. "I had a wife who stood by me and let me know that we were going to be all right. She's passed on these many years now. In one of my wiser moves, I listened to her. And you know what? At the end of those two weeks, I'd figured out what I was going to do with the rest of my life I'd always wanted to run a bookshop. Been a fool for reading since Miss Patsy turned me on to it in the first grade. I still read everything I can get my hands on.

Well, there just happened to be a bookshop in town, and the man who owned it wanted to retire.

I talked it over with my Nancy and we decided to risk a throw of the dice and take it over. It was the right roll. I suddenly found myself in the right place, doing the right thing and happier than I'd been in many, many years. My children came to the store; I could be there while they did their homework. Their friends came and brought their parents. People bought books and stayed to enjoy my Nancy's excellent fudge. We prospered. That store gave me a new life. But I would never have done it if I hadn't lost that job. Instead of coming home anxious, tired and stressed, I woke up ready to go to work and happy to do it."

"My older son David runs the shop now. After his mother died, he finished college and traveled around a bit. But in the end, he came back and asked me if he could come in with me. He'd found himself a nice young girl and had plans to marry her. When I asked him why he wanted to help run the store he said, 'I've always loved my time here. I've always loved having you around. I missed a lot of that when I was really little. I think I'd be happy working for you and maybe, eventually, take over the place when you've decided you're done.' That was good enough for me. One day I decided to turn the store over to my son. Do you know? He's never regretted that choice one, single day. And neither have I."

He paused and looked at Mitch. "All is possible, young man. Opportunities abound, but most folks just turn a blind eye when they come up. It's not the house you own, it's the people who enter it that make it a home."

Mitch was humbled and deeply moved. When he'd first met Mr. Smith, all he'd seen was a bossy old man. But listening to him now, he realized how much he would have missed if he'd stuck to that impression. And he appreciated what he was telling him. Opportunities….All is possible…where had he heard that?

Mr. Smith patted Mitch on the back and was about to get up when he noticed a folded little note sitting on his lap. He picked up the note, got up slowly and returned to where the children were noisily gardening. As he stood there, enjoying the fun the children seemed to be having, he opened his note and slowly read the curly little letters:

Your honesty, care and generosity shows people the goodness in others and in themselves.

He looked around the yard, wondering how someone could've slipped a note right onto his lap under his very nose. Then he realized, maybe it wasn't a person that did it, but a very dear, special little friend. Mr. Smith smiled, tucked the note into his shirt pocket and jumped right back into gardening with the children.

Mitch returned to his work as well, breaking up the ground with a new vigor while digesting Mr. Smith's words which left a deep impression on him. Covered in dirt from head to toe, his shirt soaking in sweat, Mitch lost all track of time, without realizing that he was nearly done.

"You can't give the ground too much water, Sylvia, or it gets mushy and muddy and it's no good. But not too little, either, or the seeds won't have anything to drink," Mr. Smith fondly reminded her. "Remember what your mama used to say about not having too much or too little?" Ms. Contadino chimed in.

"Moderation in all things," Sylvia recited.

Mr. Higgins noticed Mitch's progress and his new enthusiasm in the garden. He was swinging the hoe with a little more vigor. He patted Mitch on the back. "Good job, old boy. Sandy was right, you are a hard worker, and when you make up your mind to do something, you're unstoppable. That's a fine quality." Mr. Smith walked over to join Mitch and Mr. Higgins. The old men engaged Mitch in a lively conversation as he finished breaking the soil. They showed Mitch that a lot about life can be learned from gardening. They understood the struggles he was going through as a former breadwinner, now unemployed. They shared stories of their own poverty during the Great Depression and told Mitch of how they had managed to keep their spirits up when everyone else around them gave up. Most of all, they shared with Mitch how to see the opportunities in everything.

Watching Mitch joke with the old men stunned Sandy for a moment. She hadn't seen him so alive in such a long time. She watched him smile and laugh and furrow his brow in deep, passionate thought, and she remembered the husband she knew and loved so well. She was suddenly very thankful that she'd trusted Charlie and his grand idea. The Garden of Life—Charlie was absolutely right.

The sun was far off in the sky, preparing to set before anyone realized that it was time to go home, cook dinner and do homework. Sandy thanked Ms. Contadino and the two gentlemen, and gave big warm hugs to all the children.

"Thank you so much for helping us today," she said. "You made the work so much more fun."

"Do you, um..." the younger boy looked down at his feet. "Do you think we could come back tomorrow? I mean, if you need more help."

"I would love it. You can invite your parents, too, if you like," Sandy eagerly replied.

That night was warm, and Sandy was inside, on the couch, dozing. Mitch had gone outside so he wouldn't disturb her. They'd had an early dinner and Sandy had surprised Mitch with his favorite dessert, Key Lime Pie. He smiled to himself remembering the note he found under his plate after dinner. Sandy had picked up the dishes and didn't notice the slip of paper that had been hiding beneath his plate. As she went to get his surprise dessert, Mitch opened the note. It read:

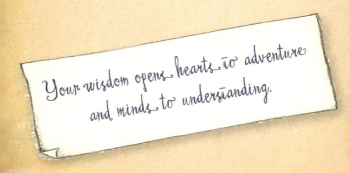

Your wisdom opens hearts to adventure and minds to understanding.

A few days ago, that note would have just frustrated Mitch even more. But today, it made him feel good about himself. It made him feel proud. Things had begun to change and he liked all of the changes. He didn't feel as stressed anymore. He was still out of work, but Sandy was right; they were making it on her salary. She'd been right about a lot of things that he hadn't wanted to admit.

That talk over dinner a couple of weeks ago had really made him think. Listening to her, he'd begun to remember what he'd been like before he'd taken the corporate job. Sure, teaching was tough, what with the district rules and the circumscribed way he'd been expected to teach his classes. And, of course, the money wasn't that great. They expected a lot out of teachers for not much pay. So when opportunity knocked, he jumped the academic ship and took the VP job. Better money, better future, bigger house… but looking back, the more they had, the more challenging life became.

There was a lot of pressure for him to succeed, and a lot of fear about losing his job if he didn't. In the end, it hadn't mattered what kind of job he was doing. The recession hit and the jobs disappeared, so had all the trappings that came with the luxurious life. It had taken both their incomes to afford the big house in the gated community, plus the car payments, yard service and pool service. All the things they were always too busy to enjoy anyway.

When Mitch and Sandy sold their home, Mitch felt as though he'd lost a large piece of himself as well. He was no longer a corporate man, and he made no money. What did that make him? The answer was simple: a loser. He watched Sandy be brave about everything, and that just seemed to make him feel worse. And the worse he felt, the worse he'd started acting. Pretty soon he didn't even recognize himself anymore.

Job offers weren't lining up for him, and the few that had come his way weren't worth taking. He still had his teaching credential. He supposed he could go back to that, but the same problems that had driven him out of the school system were still there. And Mitch had felt very, very lost and more scared than he wanted to admit to Sandy or to himself.

Inspired by Mr. Smith's words and the events of the day, Mitch realized that all that physical labor and working in the soil had refreshed his mind. He now had a new sense of clarity and began to see things differently. He was excited about working in the garden the next day, and he was looking forward to seeing everyone again.

Words of Wisdom

Charlie's Favorite Quotes

"The highest form of wisdom is kindness."
– The Talmud

"The invariable mark of wisdom is to see the miraculous in the common."
– Ralph Waldo Emerson

"A true friend sees the good in everything, and brings out the best in the worst of things."
– Sasha Azevedo

"Miracles happen to those who believe in them."
– Bernard Berenson

"Our aspirations are our possibilities."
– Samuel Johnson

"Learning is the discovery that something is possible." – Fritz Perls

"One of the greatest discoveries a man makes, one of his greatest surprises, is to find he can do what he was afraid he couldn't." – Henry Ford

"We are all faced with a series of great opportunities brilliantly disguised as impossible situations." – Charles R. Swindoll

"Whatever you can do or dream you can begin it. Boldness has genius, magic and power in it. Begin it now." – Goethe

CHAPTER SIXTEEN
A NEW PLAN FOR A NEW LIFE

*"The future belongs to those who believe
in the beauty of their dreams."* – Eleanor Roosevelt

With only one week left before the harvest feast, everyone was busily working in the garden. The children were excited for the tomatoes to mature and could barely wait to pull the purple carrots out of the ground. Mr. Smith and Mr. Higgins took the lead in making sure that all the crops would be ready for the feast, while Mitch was setting up the back porch with a long wooden table and chairs he borrowed. Sandy and Ms. Contadino were planning the menu of the feast with Charlie. Charlie was ecstatic; this was his first harvest in a very long time. It felt like Thanksgiving in the old days with Sandy's family.

In the corn patch, Sandy found a ripe ear ready to eat. She peeled away the husk and tasted it. As she took her first bite, the velvety sweetness filled her mouth.

"This corn is delicious!"

The children looked at her confused. "You can't eat corn raw!"

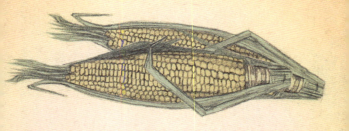

"Of course, you can. It tastes even better! Here, have a taste for yourselves!"

Soon the children were happily devouring raw ears of corn. "Raw corn really is good!"

The kids were amazed that the tiny seeds they had planted a few months ago had turned into delicious vegetables and herbs. Ms. Contadino made a treat of cucumber, tomato and basil with mozzarella on freshly baked, homemade bread sprinkled with olive oil. Everyone took a break from working in the garden to enjoy the refreshing snack. The anticipation was growing as everyone excitedly chattered about the upcoming harvest feast.

That evening, Mitch was sitting on the front porch watching the sun as it was about to set. He was reflecting on all that had recently happened. Mr. Higgins, out on his evening stroll, asked if he could join him. He had wanted to have a heart-to-heart talk with Mitch and this was the perfect time. After a brief silence, Mr. Higgins turned to Mitch. "Son, I want to thank you for what you've done here."

Mitch looked startled. "What for? What have I done?"

Mr. Higgins gestured to the yard and across to the garden. "That. That's what you've done. Do you have any idea how great that garden's been for this neighborhood? For the kids, for me, for all of us? You started something young man, whether you know it or not. These folks haven't talked in so many years; it was like meeting a whole new street full of people. That lady inside with your wife, when she lost her daughter, we all thought it was going to be the end of her. She ended up with a little granddaughter she thought she was too old to raise and she was spending her days sitting on that blasted porch of hers. Now look at her! She's in there telling your wife how to put this party thing together and planning how much food she's going to have to make! And she's loving every minute of it."

"I know a little something about them. Ms. Contadino's mother came over here from Italy. She was a fine cook. And so is Ms. Contadino. Truth to tell, part of the reason I'm making sure I can come to this

127

shindig is to taste what she makes. Been a long time, but I've got me a very good memory!" he chuckled. "You see, when you plant a garden, in the way you two planted this one, you grow so much more than plants. And you feed so much more than just the bodies who eat the fruits of what you've sown. You've grown a garden, but you've also grown and nourished people's souls. You've grown a community, knit them right back together. Taken all of us off our porches, mixed us up with the youngsters and given us a purpose, something to really look forward to. Some garden, wouldn't you say?"

Mitch didn't know how to respond. What Mr. Higgins was saying was so unexpected and, honestly, he was reluctant to take credit for something that he really hadn't wanted anything to do with in the first place. But Mr. Higgins was determined to dole out the credit where he knew the credit was due—with Mitch and Sandy.

Mitch tried to set him straight, but Mr. Higgins wasn't finished. "The garden gave new meaning to my life and I bet it did the same for others."

At that moment Mr. Smith joined them and caught the last bit of what Mr. Higgins was sharing with Mitch. "Higgins's right. The community is alive again and I feel better than ever. I feel like I have a new purpose in my life. Working with the children in the garden is the best feeling. We love those kids.

I go to bed content every night, with sore muscles sure, but feeling I did something of value. I wake every morning energized with a renewed passion for life. I love waking up and starting the day again."

"The garden is the greatest and best gift you could have ever given these two old men. Thank you."

Overwhelmed by their touching speech, Mitch looked out at the garden, finally realizing what their little project had truly become.

Meanwhile, in the garden, Charlie plucked four large arugula leaves and rinsed them in the cool stream of water that fell from the leaky hose. He carried the four delicate leaves to the front porch where Mitch, Mr. Smith and Mr. Higgins sat. After giving each man a fresh leaf, Charlie began to nibble at the edge of his leaf and his face lit up brighter and brighter with every bite. He never uttered a word, but if one simply looked at his face, he didn't have to. The three men had never seen anyone enjoy food more than this little mouse.

Charlie felt the arugula's supple, smooth texture and took a gentle whiff of its subtle fresh scent. He could smell the rich earth and the life-giving water in its cells. Each time he took a tiny nibble, he savored the tender sweetness of the leaf and the slight, nutrient-rich bitterness at its center.

Mitch's facial expressions went from confused to enthralled. Before he even took a bite, Mr. Smith knew he was going to sink his teeth into the crispest, most luscious, most delicious leaf he had ever tasted. As Mr. Higgins watched Charlie, he couldn't resist anymore so he, along with Mr. Smith, opened his mouth and took a bite.

Mitch watched as his companions ate the arugula as if they were biting into the smoothest, richest slice of chocolate cake. He finally gave in and, instantly, he understood why Sandy and the crew put so much effort into gardening. The arugula was not just arugula; it was so delicious Mitch thought he could feel the nutrients exploding in his mouth as he chewed.

It didn't have to be that only the four of them could experience the delectable joy of homegrown lettuce; all people should have this luxury.

Suddenly, like a flash of lightning, Mitch was struck with an idea! Inspired by the words of Mr. Smith and Mr. Higgins, his mind started racing a million miles a second. He realized the power of the garden to bring together a community, and he wanted every community to share in that life-changing experience.

Mitch could hardly contain his excitement as his ideas raced out of his mouth. When Sandy came out to join them, wondering what the excitement was all about, the man sitting next to her was finally the man she'd been missing for so very long. This was the Mitch she'd married. This was the man who would help change the world. Once more, she blessed Charlie. Trusting in his wisdom was one of the best things she'd ever done

It was getting dark and the conversation showed no signs of stopping. Sandy enticed them with a yummy beverage made from fresh herbs from their garden. "Come on inside. I've just prepared some iced tea from fresh mint leaves, rosemary, thyme and lemon from the garden with a hint of ginger. It's Charlie's favorite." Charlie nodded from his place on the sink board where he was enjoying his own thimbleful of iced tea. Smith turned in Charlie's direction and commented. "Good choice my friend. Excellent choice, in fact!"

Once inside, Mitch grabbed a sheet of paper and began writing in an excited frenzy, doing his best to remember everything they talked about outside. Slowly but surely, without realizing it, a business plan was taking form. Sandy glanced lovingly at Charlie, appreciating all he had done for her family. In response, Charlie pulled a piece of cheese out of his pocket with a big smile. He held it up in the air, tilted his head back and dropped the whole thing in his mouth. Sandy thought to herself, "I know, Charlie. It was the Thinking Cheese. It was always the Thinking Cheese." Then, iced tea in hand, she sat down to hear more about Mitch's exciting plan. Mitch explained to everyone that school had never been easy for him. As a young child he had been a quick learner, but after he began school, his progress was stifled. The rigid structure limited his personal development and his creativity began to suffer. He quickly lost the curiosity that made him such an eager student.

One day in high school, while taking a shortcut through the library on the way to his locker, Mitch picked up a book. It talked about different types of intelligences and new and better ways to educate students. Mitch read it and a whole new world opened up to him. He finally understood why he wasn't doing well in school.

Mitch discovered that he was one of the types who learned through real world experiences, not boring textbooks that put him to sleep. And now he knew he wasn't the only one. He then decided he wanted to support the kids in school who were more like him, and from there his journey to become a teacher began.

He began his profession with a relentless energy and enthusiasm to make a difference in the classroom. Unfortunately, the work quickly sapped him of all his energy as he became jaded with the inadequate and unresponsive education system.

But now, today, just moments before, Mitch realized that gardening could be a powerful teaching environment. The classroom would be in the garden, and the teachers would be experienced retired senior citizens with valuable life lessons to offer. Students who have difficulty in the traditional classroom would thrive in such an environment where they would learn hands-on with the warmth and wisdom of a teacher-mentor.

While budget concerns were a headache for the traditional school system, Mitch's model would be free of such issues, because healthy food would be grown for not only the students and teachers but also the whole community. There would be no more budget concerns and even landowners would benefit from having their vacant weed-filled lots maintained. The students would get a better education at a fraction of the cost. The seniors who serve as teacher-mentors would have a new fulfilling and purposeful life as they became vital in contributing to society for everyone's benefit. Beautiful gardens would fill communities across the nation and everyone would be able to take part in the efforts.

Students would learn useful life skills such as growing food, the value of hard work and knowledge regarding nutrition and exercise. As they worked in the garden, their creativity and independent thinking skills would be encouraged. They would also develop entrepreneurial skills in addition to learning math, history, the arts and sciences. Lessons learned in the garden would be practical life lessons, giving the students a great foundation for their futures.

Everyone's face lit up as they were overjoyed to see the changes in Mitch's attitude. They knowingly winked at each other as Mitch, without even noticing, continued outlining his plan. As Sandy watched Mitch speak with joy and newfound energy, she was reminded of the Mitch that she first met. This was the Mitch that loved life and it was obvious to everyone.

"We will create a comprehensive education plan that will work powerfully to transform and reunite our nation's communities by feeding and nourishing all its citizens. It will awaken our spirits so that we can embrace the original values for which this great country was founded," Mitch stated, triumphantly.

Mr. Smith, Mr. Higgins, Sandy and Charlie all applauded as Mitch finished his ambitious plan.

Mitch could no longer think about a bigger house or finding a better job. He was on a mission and he was unstoppable. His passion and contagious enthusiasm inspired everyone around him. For Sandy, the transformation was deeply moving and profound. Mitch had come so far in just a few short weeks, and she was excited again about their new life together.

The group decided to launch their plans at the harvest party. Mitch asked all of the neighborhood kids and seniors to create and distribute flyers announcing the event. Mitch also contacted local newspapers, radio stations and even TV stations. He poured all his heart, passion and energy into making the launch a big success.

The morning of the harvest party, as the whole neighborhood slept, Mitch and Sandy worked in their kitchen putting the finishing touches on their plans for the day. Charlie sat nearby, watching two of his favorite people as he juggled a piece of Thinking Cheese between his paws.

Sensing his presence, Sandy turned to see Charlie in his familiar thinking pose. Mitch turned to join her, putting his arm affectionately around his wife's shoulders. Taking a sip of hot tea made with herbs from their garden, Mitch asked, "What do you think he's planning for us now?"

"I have no idea," Sandy replied with a knowing smile, "but I can't wait to find out!"

All is Possible
- Charlie

Words of Wisdom
Charlie's Favorite Quotes

"Just don't give up on trying to do what you really want to do. Where there is love and inspiration, I don't think you can go wrong."
– Ella Fitzgerald

"Do not quench your inspiration and your imagination." – Vincent Van Gogh

"I am not afraid of tomorrow, for I have seen yesterday and I love today."
– William Allen White

"I like the dreams of the future better than the history of the past" – Thomas Jefferson

"To find your own way is to follow your bliss. This involves analysis, watching yourself and seeing where real deep bliss is -- not the quick little excitement , but the real deep, life-filling bliss." – Joseph Campbell

"The glory of friendship is not the outstretched hand, nor the kindly smile, nor the joy of companionship; it's the spiritual inspiration that comes to one when he discovers that someone else believes in him and is willing to trust him with his friend." – Fritz Perls

"Get excited and enthusiastic about you own dream. This excitement is like a forest fire - you can smell it, taste it, and see it from a mile away." – Denis Waitley

About the Author

Mark Juarez overcame dyslexia and all the subsequent challenges at school to become a successful businessman and passionate entrepreneur.

At the age of 11, he started his first business mowing lawns until he began to notice that many houses in his neighborhood were in disrepair. Realizing the owners were living on a fixed income and unable to afford expensive contractors, Mark offered to do the repairs at a very low cost and his business soon grew. He put on new roofs, replaced broken windows and doors, patched holes in walls and painted the inside and outside of houses. Mark refused to take payment until the clients were completely satisfied and found ways to accommodate even the smallest budget. So began an incredible, and dignified, work ethic that has continued to this day.

At the age of 18, he gave up his business for a corporate job and quickly climbed the proverbial ladder. By the age of 21, he became so disillusioned with corporate America that he set out on a journey of self-discovery and exploration.

This journey took him all around the world for 10 years as he experienced different cultures and the rich diversities they offered. With a compassionate heart and an overwhelming desire to help make the world a better place, he learned to think with his heart, listen to his instincts, follow his passions and, most importantly, act upon his dreams.

During his many years of travel, he set out on an around-the-world bicycle expedition from San Francisco to raise awareness against nuclear proliferation and to advance aid in helping the hungry and homeless. He made it all the way to Europe before suffering a knee injury which prompted him to try massage as a way of healing. It worked so well that he went on to become a massage therapist, where he discovered that hands could become an extension of the heart.

With the realization that a caring touch could make an incredible difference in people's lives, The Happy Company was born to produce the Happy Massager.

The Happy Company was created through the coming together of people who share Mark's vision of making a positive difference in the world. The two most important philosophies of The Happy Company are "Integrity Before Profit" and "Work Is Love Made Visible." The Happy Company has sold over 10 million Happy Massagers, make it the world's best selling, and most beloved, massage tool.

Mark is an entrepreneur, a world traveler, a CEO, an inventor, a designer, an avid cyclist, a teacher, a certified masseuse and a public speaker. He is also well known for his ability to successfully innovate and create new products with 'character.'

Additionally, over the last 5 years, he has been designing a revolutionary, environmentally conscious way to build houses that are less expensive, more efficient and more sustainable. His methods are safer than conventional houses, will last longer, require less maintenance, will sustain less damage in fire & earthquakes and are still aesthetically pleasing.

The character of Charlie was born from a powerful concern about the impact the current financial conditions are having on everyday life. The book's message comes from Mark's deep-seated belief that, no matter what, All is Possible.

Mark recognizes the correlation between past and present day struggles, and hopes we might learn from both. A goal of this story is to open the dialogue between generations and instill in others the principle of looking for opportunity in all circumstances.

ALL IS POSSIBLE!!!

ACKNOWLEDGMENTS

I believe that our lives are shaped by our life experiences and the people we meet. This book was written as a reflection of my life experiences and all the amazing people I have been privileged enough to meet. I am incredibly grateful for the generosity and support of so many people who share this vision and truly see the positive impact this book will have on all who read it. It is because of their continual encouragement and assistance this dream has been realized.

I have so many people to thank:

Assistance in writing, creative input & editing: Reese Leyva, Jennifer Arnold, Terri Renfro, Leah Li, Lucineida Fonseca, Sharon Ma, Rebekka Bruhn, and Shannon Burke Special thanks to Jennifer who helped me lay the foundation of the book and brought the characters to life. Thanks also to Reese, who with her unwavering enthusiasm helped to beautifully articulare the story.

Art design and direction: Heidi Woehrle, Cheryl Isaacson, Joel Judal
Special thanks to Heidi and Cheryl for their patience and generous creative input that made the book come alive.

Illustration: Michael Fravel, Kledy Dongo Pflucker
Thanks to Michael for capturing the true essence of
Charlie.

Editing: Linda Heckt, Andrea Glass

The amazing staff of The Happy Company: Cindy Souza,
Liz Schleth, Barbara Boje, Mela McGary, Sharon Ma,
Ingrid Pauselius, Patty Corona, Amy Liu, Joyce Zhao,
Minh Truong, Ed Protiva, Jack Gibson
Special thanks to everyone for their loyal support and valu-
able input and for making this book a reality. Thanks for
making the Happy Company extraordinary. I'm incredibly
grateful to all of you.

My Neighbors and Friends: Bob & Joan Boyen, Mike &
Rosa Munnelly, Jerry & Jeanne Woods, Donald Fitzgerald,
Elke Ney Murphy, Krystal Niu, Anna Ling Jin

The greatest treasures in my life are my family, friends, and
neighbors. For in the end they are all that matters.

There are so many others who have contributed to my life
and the book in so many ways and I am truly grateful.